Rag Rugs

Rag Rugs

Ann Davies

The Art of Crafts

First published in 1999 by
The Crowood Press Ltd
Ramsbury, Marlborough
Wiltshire SN8 2HR

British Library Cataloguing-in-Publication Data

A catalogue record for this book is available from the British Library.

ISBN 1 86126 229 9

Picture credits: Title page: Hooked rug 1930s. (Reproduced by permission of the Museum of Welsh Life, St. Fagans, Cardiff). Frontispiece: Strelitza (Hilary Ansell). Photo Christine Carpenter.

Dedicated to my late husband, Neil, who encouraged me to explore my craft, and to my good friends Milly and Brian Smith.

Grateful thanks to Mary and John Bell for all their support and helpful comments; to Hillary Ansell, Mary Dayton, Tessa Miller, Margaret Walker, and Pat Willis for so kindly agreeing to let me show examples of their work; and to Neville Smith for crafting so many of the tools illustrated. Also Linton Tweeds, Cloth Market of Stamford, Texere, and Colinette Yarns for their beautiful tweeds, materials and yarns which have been incorporated into some of my work. Also thanks to the National Trust, and the Museum of Welsh Life, St. Fagans, Cardiff, for giving me permission to reproduce rugs in their collections. Also to my students who, over the years, have asked awkward questions to which I had to find the answers.

Typeface used: Melior

Designed and typeset by Focus Publishing, Sevenoaks, Kent

Printed and bound by Leo Paper Products, China

Contents

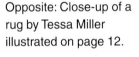

Introduction

The making of rag rugs – or mats as they are known in various parts of the British Isles – is a traditional craft which has passed through periods of popularity from the late 1880s to the present day. Basically the two traditional and better known rag rug techniques are known as 'hooky' and 'proddy', or 'hooking' and 'prodding'. The hooking method is the one most practised in both North America and the United Kingdom.

Hooky rugs are made using an implement which is like a crochet hook, but the hook is much more acute, and the shank is shaped and held with a wooden handle. Nowadays there are three sizes: all purpose, intermediate and fine. The first is the one most often used, and as its name suggests, it is a good general purpose tool; the other two are for finer cuts of fabric or yarn – the fine hook can even be used with embroidery threads. In this technique the hook is pushed firmly through a base fabric, usually hessian (burlap), which has been stretched tautly over a frame, and catches part of a strip of material held between the finger and thumb underneath the base fabric; it is then pulled back up so that the material forms a loop on the right side of the material. In earlier times hooks were home-made; they were usually heavier and chunkier than modern-day tools as they were often used in conjunction with sacking, which had a very loose weave; the strips of material therefore had to be cut wider to fill the loose mesh. Hooks were made in a variety of shapes and sizes, using what was available to the maker; for instance some were all metal, and others were metal with wooden handles. They ranged from being made with a nail with a V roughly cut at the top, to machine-turned tools.

In the 'proddy' technique, short lengths of material are pushed through a base fabric (again usually hessian) from the reverse side using a prodder, a wooden implement shaped to a point at one end; it does not have a hook. Sometimes an awl was used. Two contemporary versions are shown on page 9, one of which has a brass shank and yew handle. It is up to you which you use; I prefer the wooden implement. The base fabric can be either stretched on a frame or held in your lap. This way of making rugs produces a shaggy pile,

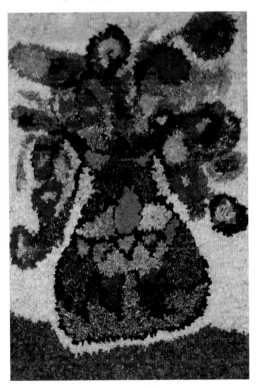

Opposite: Close-up of a rug by Tessa Miller illustrated on page 12.

Left: Modern hanging made in Cuba. Loops hooked and then cut.

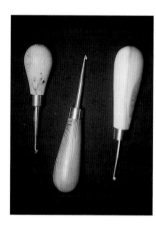

Top: New hooks - from left to right: General purpose, Intermediate, Fine.

Centre: Selection of old hooks.

Right: Selection of old prodders.

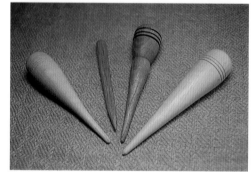

and is the one which many people traditionally associate with the term 'rag rug'. In earlier times the base was loose-weave sacking, and this meant that the pieces of material had to be cut very wide, in order to remain lodged in the sacking. As a result a completed rug was very heavy, and many a tale is told concerning the effort involved in handling them – impossible to shake, they were generally dragged out of doors and hung over the washing line, and then beaten with a carpet beater, and if they had to be washed they became even heavier, and took days to dry out.

The introduction of a new rug was quite an occasion, as it generally upstaged more than one other. Sometimes it was used as a bedcover before being put on the floor but, if intended for the floor, it would be placed in front of the hearth in the main living area. The old rug was put into the scullery, and the rug from there was sometimes put into the outdoor lavatory or dog kennel; the oldest rug from the latter was then thrown away.

The two terms 'hooky' and 'proddy' both have regional variations; for instance, 'pegged' or 'poked' was sometimes used for proddy because the implement used was often part of an old-fashioned wooden clothes peg whittled down to make a point, or even just a whittled piece of wood, and the fabric pieces were poked through the sacking. How exactly rag rug making began is a point of contention, since claims to its origins are made on both sides of the Atlantic both by the United Kingdom and North America. Unfortunately its history is not well documented as it was considered a 'working class' craft, and not worthy of being included in the numerous books on handicrafts and embroidery produced during the late Victorian era. Although it is claimed that the incorporation of loops into a textile goes back as far as the Copts, its precise origins are not known. In an authoritative book entitled *The Hooked Rug*, published in 1937, William Winthrop Kent, an American architect, was in correspondence with Ann Macbeth, a well known craftswoman in the United Kingdom, at one time Chief Instructress at the Glasgow School of Art, and author of many books on crafts and the teaching of embroidery. It was her contention that the making of rugs was peculiarly the heritage of the Celto-Scandinavian countries, and she restated this belief in her book *The Country Woman's Rug Book*. Some North American textile authorities claim it originated in their maritime provinces and was the result of immigrants seeing sailors using a marlin spike, a piece of equipment with a form of hook at one end used for making ropes. As well as the

United States and Britain, rug making was, and still is, carried out in various parts of Canada, especially in Ontario, Labrador, Newfoundland and Nova Scotia. (In Newfoundland hessian is sometimes called brin.) Whatever the theories, its origins are open to speculation.

On a recent visit to Bulgaria I went to a craft exhibition, and there I saw a rag wall hanging which had been made in Cuba. It was done by the hooked technique, though the loops had been cut. The obvious connection here was the United States of America, only a short distance away.

Hooked rag rugs were popular in North America in the mid- to late nineteenth century, and on the whole the standard of both colour and design was greatly superior to that in the rugs being worked in Great Britain at the same time. British rugs tended to be utilitarian, largely because the clothing worn typically in those days was mainly dark in order not to show the dirt so much: these colours were therefore predominant in the rugs. Many of them would have a wide dark border. The rug shown here to illustrate this feature is a copy of an old rug which belonged at Smallhythe Place, managed by the National Trust. The old rug was very faded and worn; however, it was lined on the reverse and, on removing the lining, the original colours were found to be very bright and lively. The Trust decided that they wanted the colours to be depicted as they would originally have appeared, and I was commissioned to make the copy for them; it was a fascinating project to carry out.

Of course there are always exceptions to every trend, and certainly mats bright in colour and of particularly good design were made, and these were obviously treasured by their makers and their families. Examples of these can be seen

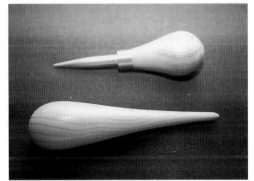

Above: Rug commissioned from the author by the National Trust. A copy of a rug in Smallhythe Place, Kent. (Reproduced by permission of The National Trust.)

Left: New prodders: top brass and yew, bottom yew wood.

in various folk museums throughout the British Isles. One such exception is illustrated here: it was made in Wales in the early part of the twentieth century and demonstrates a remarkable appreciation of design and colour, as seen in the close-up opposite. A proddy mat from the same source is also highly exuberant in its use of colour. It is interesting that there is evidence of rags being employed in rug making elsewhere in Europe, though tools were not generally used; more commonly rags were woven into rugs, table runners, cushions and so on.

Also, it would seem that people in the islands of the Caribbean have been busy with a form of rag rugging for some considerable time: rice sacks and a fine hairpin were used to make a looped rag rug, and the loops were then cut.

In this latter part of the twentieth century, rag rug making has come a long way from the original concept of having something warm on which to put your feet. More recently textile artists have discovered its possibilities, and have incorporated its techniques into all sorts of textile disciplines. The original concept of recyling unwanted materials has not been ignored, since many different kinds of scrap material are used, both natural and man-made; and nowadays the craft encompasses the making of a wide variety of objects, not just rugs – these include wallhangings, cushion covers, bags, seat covers, mirror surrounds, clothing, seat pads – the list is endless!

We have already discussed the hand-held tools used in the two traditional methods of rag rug making, but other implements have been developed along with these over the years. In the 1920s and 1930s there was a variety of patent gadgets on the market, for instance the 'Airlyne' machine: this was clamped to a

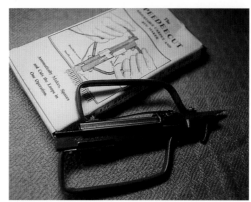

Top left: The 'Handee' tool (1930s) showing the three components: razor blade, needle and hook.

Top right: Two Airlyne machines (1930s showing the braid foot control fixed to the underside of the machine, and the position of the needle.

Bottom left: The 'Speedecut' Rugmaker (1930s).

table and operated by a foot control. A large pointed needle passed through an aperture in the centre of a platform; fitted to the underside of the machine was a spring device, to which was attached a strong braid with a loop at the bottom. The worker's foot was slipped into the loop, and as he moved it up and down, so the needle moved. Hessian was the base fabric: it was held tautly over the needle with the design uppermost, and the worker moved it over the needle. It was claimed that one hundred loops a minute could be formed. Rug wool (yarn) was recommended for use with this machine.

Other gadgets in use included the 'Handee Rug-Making Tool', which its manufacturers claimed to be '...the only rug-making tool which knots, gauges and cuts in one simple operation'; it was worked on canvas and the cutting gauge was a razor-blade, and it was suggested that '...those [blades] discarded for shaving are adequate refills for the Rug

Opposite: Close up of a motif from the rug shown on page 12.

Right: Hooked rug 1930s.
(Reproduced by
permission of the
Museum of Welsh Life,
St. Fagans, Cardiff).

Opposite: Prodded rug.
Welsh. Date unknown.
(Reproduced by
permission of the
Museum of Welsh Life,
St. Fagans, Cardiff.)

Tool'. There was also the 'Speedecut Rugmaker' which claimed to make, space and cut the loops in one automatic operation; like the previous two gadgets, rug wool was the suggested yarn. The instructions do not specify the base fabric to be used, but it is assumed it would be hessian. As the gadget incorporated scissors to cut the loops (and not a razor blade, as with the 'Handee' tool), the manufacturers offered a grinding /sharpening service. There was another similar device called the 'Emu High Speed Rug Maker', and yet more gadgets were illustrated in various books and magazines of the period, though not all have stood the test of time. The ones that are still with us are the rugger, the punch needle, the locker hook, the latch hook and the shuttle hook.

Right: Mixed-media
hanging, inspired by
Persian and Turkish
carpets. The base
fabric was Helsinki
furnishing fabric dyed in
the washing machine.
The embroidered panels
are on a base fabric of
dyed calico, machine
embroidered strips of
various silks, muslin,
chiffon, organza and
polyester, which have
been cut out and applied
to the base fabric. The
background is hooking.
(Worked by Tessa Miller).
Photo Christine Carpenter

In this book we will look at two of the traditional techniques, namely hooking and prodding, and their application today; then we shall cover some of the less well known, such as the speed needle, the rugger and the locker needle; and finally we will introduce two new implements, the giant lucet and the looper. We will consider how the hooking technique can be used on its own, or adapted for use with other textile techniques; and also how the loop can be used in a non-traditional way.

1 Materials and Tools

BASE FABRICS

The base fabrics used in the various techniques illustrated in this book are as follows:

Hessian

This comes in two weights: 12oz and 10oz. The 12oz hessian has a finer weave and is of better quality than the 10oz; it is used mainly for hooking and fine prodding.

The 10oz hessian is much coarser and looser in weave and can be used for heavier hooking, prodding, and with the rugger and the looper.

When purchasing hessian make sure that it has not been treated with a flame retardant. If a material is likely to be used for upholstery purposes EC regulations specify that it must be conditioned in this way in order to prevent the risk of fire in the home. However, the treatment will make hessian very stiff, and then it is difficult to push an implement through the mesh.

Grey Polyester

This fabric is man-made and always grey in colour; it is used in the carpet industry. It is evenly woven and easy to work on, but is more expensive than hessian. It is an excellent alternative for those who may be allergic to hessian, and can be used instead of it in conjunction with the hook, prodder and looper. It is also ideal for the speed needle.

Canvas

This is a single-weave square mesh which comes in a variety of counts (squares) to the inch: the higher the number, the finer the canvas.

In rag rug making usually three counts are used: 3.3 squares to the inch (used for locker hooking, the rugger and the looper); 5 squares to the inch (used for locker hooking) and 7 squares to the inch (used with a fine locker needle).

Materials Used on the Base Fabric

Traditionally, woollen materials were widely used in the production of various kinds of rag rug, bearing in mind that the majority of man-made materials have only come onto the market during the twentieth century. Before this, most of the clothes worn were made of wool and cotton, and so these were the main fabrics used by the early rug makers.

The clothes available were generally utilitarian and dark, although red was sometimes obtainable in discarded army

Below: Canvas. From top to bottom: 3.3 squares to the inch, 5 squares to the inch, 7 squares to the inch.

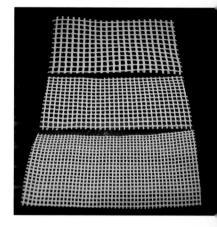

Left: Base fabrics: From top to bottom: 12 oz hessian, grey polyester, 10 oz hessian.

Opposite: Some of the materials that can be used in the making of rag rugs: chiffon, lurex, velvet, wool, netting, silk paper, silk, organza, tweed, cotton.

Right: Strelitza (30 x 31in / 76 x 80 cm). Border and black outlines hooked in black fabric; the rest of the hanging uses a variety of plastic bags.(Hilary Ansell). Photo Christine Carpenter.

uniforms. Everything was utilized, particularly during World War II when the virtues of the motto 'make do and mend' were extolled: at this time a variety of materials, including rayon stockings, parachute silk, interlock vests, thick rug yarn, as well as more traditional materials, were incorporated into rugs.

Nowadays things have changed, and we have an abundance of fabrics and yarns of every kind. It is interesting to imagine what our ancestors would have made of the variety of fabrics and yarns available to the textile enthusiast of today. Woollen material is still one of my favourites, however, and I will go out of my way to search out and buy close-weave 100 per cent woollen blankets. Unfortunately, as people increasingly use duvets in the home, wool blankets are becoming hard to find, and it is very expensive to buy pure new wool flannel, although it is obtainable.

Other fabrics are available however, and jersey fabric, felted jumpers and T-shirts, and a whole variety of other materials and yarns can be employed for rag rugs. For the more fanciful, and if

you don't have to worry about the wearing qualities of the article you are making, it is quite conceivable to use velvets of all kinds (particularly stretch velvets), velours, silks, crimplene, hand-dyed paper, raffia, florist's paper, ribbons of every description, plastic bags in every colour and hue, terry towelling, net, organza and lurex. It is interesting to see how fabrics alter their appearance when used in different rug-making techniques.

Although in this book most of the examples shown are worked with fabric, both factory-made and hand-spun yarns can be used. In the main it is better if the yarns are thickly spun.

In nearly every case the material should be cut on the straight and parallel with the selvage. Obviously, if you are cutting up scraps the selvage is not always indicated, but even so, try and cut your strips as much on the straight of the grain as possible.

Whatever materials you use, bear in mind the wearing qualities of the fabric or yarn you have chosen. Very much depends on what you are making and, in the case of a rug, where is it going to be placed; so for instance, avoid using silks and velvets in a rug destined for a heavily used area. Nowadays textile artists use a variety of materials, both

Below: Small rug worked entirely with plastic bags. (Carole Purchase)

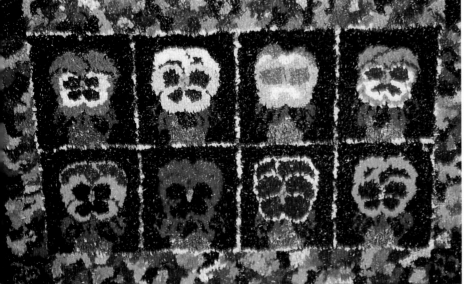

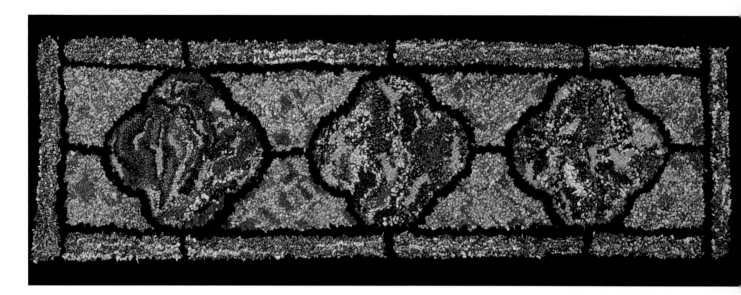

natural and man-made, and as long as the pile is well packed, the fibres can work well together.

Examples of rugs and hangings using a variety of plastic bags are shown here, and these make a perfect recycling project. On the whole you need to cut the strips wider than for conventional materials, although this depends on the type of bag you are cutting up: thus flimsy market-stall bags would need to be cut into wider strips than sturdier carrier bags. Black bin liners vary in quality, and you would need to cut the strips according to the weight of the plastic. If the finished article is to be used as a rug you would have to consider the type of wear it would receive: for instance, if it is for bathroom use, then it would be advisable to use a base fabric such as grey polyester or even-weave curtaining material rather than hessian, as these will more easily withstand damp. You can, of course, mix plastic and other fabrics and techniques together, and some of the pieces illustrated show this.

Also shown is a sampler in the process of being worked, using the hooking technique. Many different fabrics, both natural and man-made,

have been tried out, and in fact this project might be considered an experimental exercise in recyling – you will see in the picture below some of the materials that have been used. The circles into which the fabrics have been hooked are from plastic bottle tops, with yarn stitched over them.

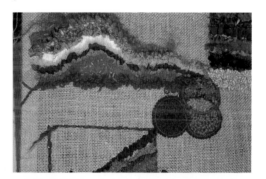

Above: Stained glass runner inspired by a visit to La Sainte Chapelle, Paris. Border and black outline hooked in black fabric; remainder hooked with a variety of plastic bags. (Hilary Ansell). Photo Christine Carpenter.

Hooked sampler showing the effects produced by using a variety of fabrics and recycled yarns. (Mary Dayton)

Towelling, knitting yarns, fabric, ribbon and paper used in the above sampler.

As with plastic bags discussed above, how wide you cut the fabric strips depends on the nature of the materials you intend to use for the hooking and prodding, and also on the base fabric. Thus, if you use a 12oz hessian you can cut finer strips than if you are using a 10oz hessian, as the strips will be trapped and held in place more firmly. Also thicker fabrics should be cut into finer strips than less substantial fabrics such as silk and net. You can hook very fine strips with a finer hook, and using a material base such as linen or an even-weave fabric.

It isn't easy to estimate how much material you will need to cover a certain area. The best way to work this out is to cut a 15in strip to the width you were intending to hook with, and then hook this strip on a practice frame. Measure the length of hooking on the hessian, and the measurement of the completed strip will show you how many loops the strip will make. You then multiply this by the fabric you wish to use. A practice frame is also useful if you want to see what a

Above: Vase of flowers
(24 x 35in / 61 x 87 cm)
Background and part of vase: hooked plastic bags; flowers in a variety of techniques and using nets, plastic bags, crimplene and T-shirting; leaves hooked using T-shirt material.
(Hilary Ansell). Photo Christine Carpenter.

Right: Close-up of some of the flowers.

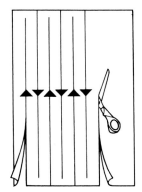 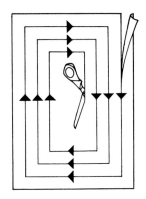 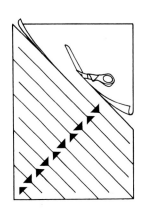 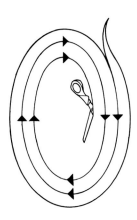

material looks like when it is hooked – by working just a small area you can see if you like it and if it is going to work, and if it isn't, you can discard the idea and so save a lot of time and effort.

Another rule of thumb used in connection with woollen material is, if you fold your piece of fabric into four and place it on the base hessian, the area covered by the folded piece will be roughly the area of hooking. Of course much will depend on how high or low you hook your loops.

To obtain longer strips and obviate too much joining, you can cut your material in a continuous strip. As you will see from the sketches above, there are various ways in which this can be done. In diagram 1, the strips are cut straight: cut in the direction of the arrows, but stop cutting a short way from the edge, leaving just enough fabric to stop the strips coming apart. Then cut the second strip parallel to the first strip at whatever width you wish it to be. Continue in this way across the fabric. If you are cutting strips for the looper and speed needle, they need to be quite thin; for the giant lucet they will need to be much wider. Alternatively, you can cut your material in a square towards the centre. If you want to cut your strips on the bias for locker needle, then follow the same procedure as for the straight strips – that

is, not through to the edge on every other row.

In many North American books a material called monkscloth is mentioned: this is not available in the United Kingdom, but grey polyester will work just as well.

TOOLS

Depending on the technique you wish to pursue, and in addition to the tool you are going to use, you basically require a pair of scissors, a simple frame, if applicable (either a picture frame or artists' stretchers – or you can make one yourself, although do make sure the corners are very firm) a staple gun and staples. Staple guns are now relatively inexpensive and save a great deal of effort. Drawing pins (thumbtacks) can be used in place of staples, but they do have a tendency to pop out when continuous pressure is put on the base fabric. If you wish to use other implements to assist you they are available, but if you want to keep this activity as a thrift craft the list given above is all you need.

The additional aids which help speed up the preparation procedure are namely a rotary cutter, a self-sealing mat for use with the cutter, and a metal-edged ruler or shape-cut grid: these are a great help in cutting strips.

Above: Sketch showing various ways of cutting strips following the direction of the arrows.

Rotary Cutters

These come in various shapes, but all consist of a handle with a cutting wheel at one end, the wheel completely covered by a guard: when you retract the guard, your wheel is ready to cut your material. Remember, this is a very sharp piece of equipment, therefore always cut away from you. You need to hold the grid or ruler firmly down on the fabric, always ensuring that you keep your hand at a distance from the cutter in case the latter slips. Get into the habit of immediately snapping the blade guard into position whenever you put the cutter aside: it is essential that you do this every time. Following these simple guidelines will mean you can use a useful tool safely and wisely.

There are various rotary cutters on the market, and it is a matter of personal

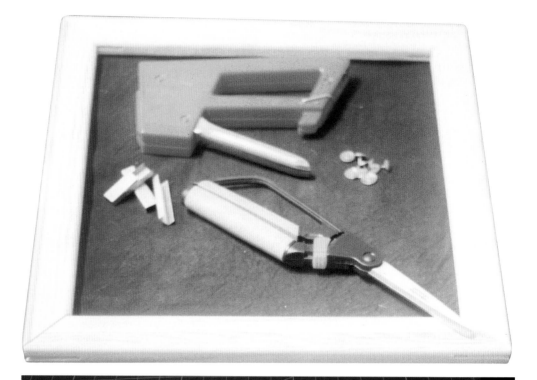

Right: Scissors, simple frames (picture frame or artists' stretchers) staple gun and staples, drawing pins. Photo Christine Carpenter.

Right: Rotary cutter and replacement blade, self-sealing mat and metal-edged ruler. Photo Christine Carpenter.

preference which one you use; I like one that fits snugly into the hand. A rotary cutter blade should be tight, but not too tight: tightening the nut too much will make the blade difficult to work with. The blades should last a long time, but if you do have to replace them, new ones are readily available and easily fitted to the cutter by a screw; alternatively there are agencies who will sharpen blades for you. Make sure that when you discard a blade, you dispose of it very carefully.

The Self-Sealing Mat

This is exactly what its name implies: when you cut on it with your rotary cutter, the cut that you make reseals itself. The mat has a square grid printed on it so you can line your material up on the straight; then, with a ruler that has a protective metal edge, run the cutter up along the material, away from you, not towards you.

The Shape Cut

I also use a grid called a 'shape cut': this is made of thick, clear plastic and has measurements printed on it, similar to the cutting mat. It comes with full instructions for its operation and is very simple to use. It has pre-cut slits in it, and an indentation at each end of the strip in which you place the blade of the rotary cutter. Guide the rotary cutter into the base of the slit and, using the slit as a guide, push the cutter up its length. Continue doing this along the width of the grid, or as wide as the material goes. For the sake of expediency you can fold your material, usually double if you are using wool, and three or four times with a lighter fabric. The cutter will cut multiple strips from ⅛in up to 12in, in ½in increments. Narrower strips can be cut by carefully moving the grid so that the two cut edges are halfway beneath the grid and then cutting up the slit; this

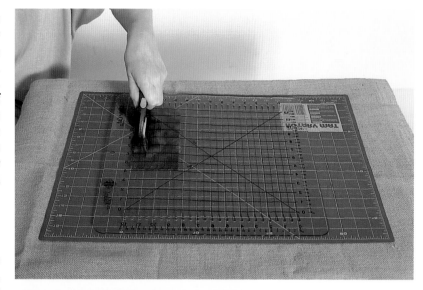

Above: Using the shape cut: self-sealing mat, shape cut, rotary cutter. Photo Christine Carpenter.

Left: Trestles and G-clamps.

gives you ¼in strips. When you first use the shape cut, spray onto its reverse surface a short burst of the sort of adhesive which allows for repositioning paper and photographs; this will prevent it slipping whilst strips are being cut. It will remain slightly tacky, and there is generally no need to respray. Alternatively you can abrade the reverse surface with some sandpaper so as to roughen it slightly; this will also prevent it slipping about. If you don't want to use a rotary cutter, then you will need a good pair of sharp scissors.

In North America there are several machines available which will cut multiple strips mechanically; however, they are generally expensive to import into the United Kingdom.

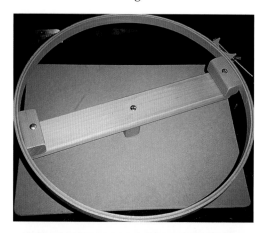

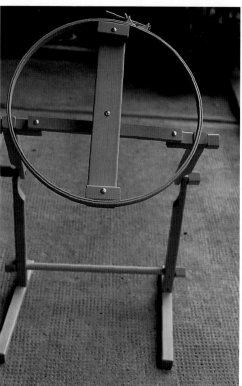

Top right: Circular frame which moves round 360 degrees. Specially made for rug makers. Table mounted. (BWH Designs).

Bottom right: The same frame floor mounted. (BWH Designs).

THE WORKING ENVIRONMENT

With any craftwork, good lighting and comfortable surroundings are important. Note, too, that whenever you become seriously immersed in your work it is very tempting to continue for too long. To avoid back and wrist strain, take a break every half an hour or so: stand up and look at your work, go and make a drink, do anything just to have a short respite – or change to another piece of work using a different technique.

Have your frame on two supports – either trestles, or across the arms of an armchair – or lean it against a table. Make sure you are sitting comfortably. Lighting is important: you need to see what you are doing clearly. If you use trestles, fix the frame onto them with four G-clamps. G-clamps are also useful for fixing small frames to a table or other surface. Have your materials close at hand: I use a laundry bag on a stand to hold my current collection. And after you have cut them up, put the strips into clear polythene bags so they can be seen easily and are kept together.

FRAMES

To start with you have a choice: you can use an old picture frame, although this must be sturdy enough to take staples or drawing pins (thumbtacks), and it must be well put together at the corners; or you can use artists' stretchers, which are readily available in art supply shops and come in a variety of lengths from 6in up to at least 50in. The corners are ready mitred and easy to assemble, although initially you may find they need a little assistance to come together – a sharp tap with another piece of wood or a bang on the table will often help to make them fit in. When using a fixed frame of this type with hessian stretched over it, bear in

mind that you often have to hold one hand underneath it, so a width of no more than 28in is advisable. You can work to any length. For ease of working, picture frames and small frames can be clamped to a table with G-clamps – and when purchasing the latter, be sure to select ones that will allow for the thickness of your table, plus the depth of your frame.

For those who wish to work a piece larger than 28in wide, there are specialist frames available.

One such looks very similar to an embroidery slate frame, but instead of having a strong braid at top and bottom on to which you sew your fabric, the top and bottom pieces have a channel grooved through them, and dowelling holds the base fabric: your hessian is turned down at top and bottom along the width and stitched to make a hem, then a piece of dowelling is pushed through each hem. The dowelling and hessian together are guided through the channels. Two side pieces are then pushed through the gaps at either end of the top and bottom pieces, and held by wooden pegs. This method enables you to work a longer article by rolling your base fabric round the top and bottom rollers. The frames come in various widths from 28in inside

Above: Component parts of the frame, similar to an embroidery slate frame, but using dowelling to hold the base fabric. (Spindlewood Turnery).

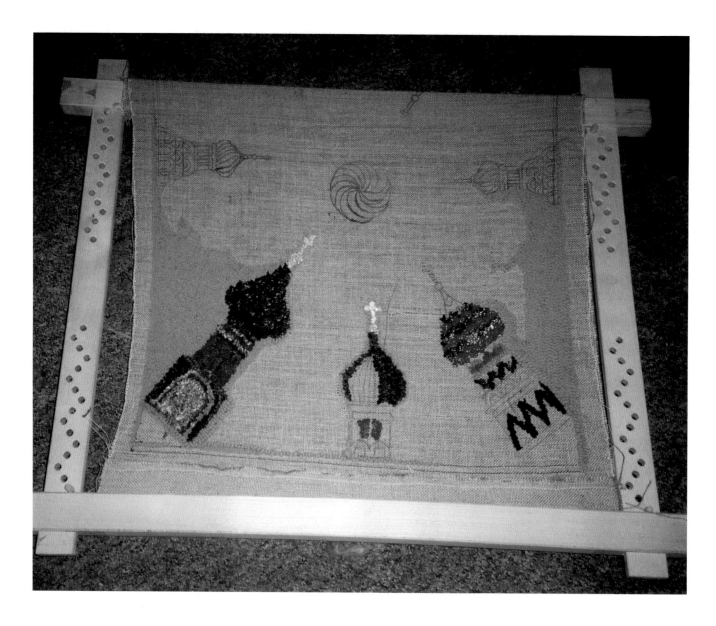

Above: Work stretched on
the frame.

measurement (the length of the dowel)
up to 50in.

Also illustrated is a ring similar to an
embroidery or quilting hoop, but with a
larger diameter. It comes supplied with
a screw on the outer ring, long enough
to accommodate the thickness of the
worked area of the rug. It is available as
a table model or with a floor stand, and
swivels through 360 degrees for easy
access to the part of the rug you are

working on. When using this type of
frame it is advisable to loosen off the
tension on the screw after each work
session, because this prevents the loops
from becoming too flattened – although
having said that, most fabrics will
spring back easily.

There is also the extremely well made
floor standing frame known as the
Lowery frame, named after its makers:
this model uses dowels and hemmed

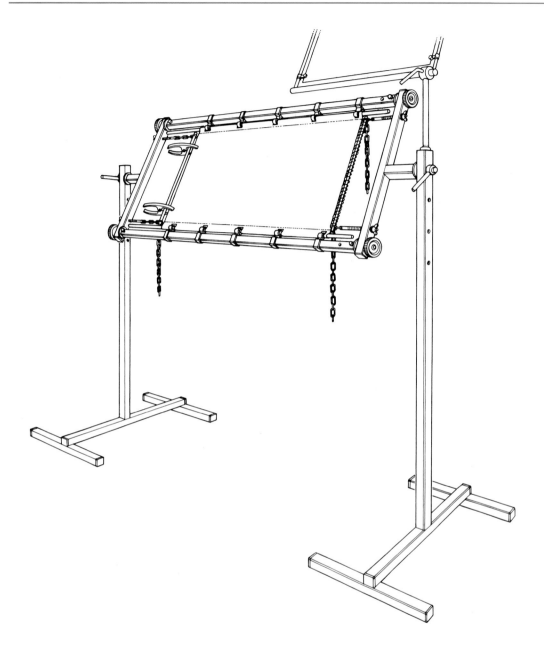

material too, but the dowelling is outside the top and bottom of the frame; the fabric is kept taut by the use of strong clips and chains which are supplied with the frame. It takes to pieces for storage.

To sum up: start with an old picture frame or artists' stretchers, and as you progress, go on to other frames. If you just do not wish to handle a large frame you can always do your work in sections and sew the pieces together afterwards; however, if you do this you will certainly have a weakness where the seams are, and the article will not be as long wearing.

Above: Lowery Workshops floor-mounted frame.

2 Colour and Dyeing

Colour is an emotive subject. We talk of being 'red with anger', 'blue with cold', 'green with envy', and of 'cowardly yellow'. Colour can convey moods, ideas, warmth and coolness, and it is essentially a very personal thing.

Colour pigments consist of three primary colours: red, yellow and blue, and they are called primary because they cannot be obtained by mixing other colours together. Next come three secondary pigments, namely orange, green and violet, each the result of two primary colours being mixed together; and then three tertiary pigments which are the result of mixing equal quantities of a primary and a secondary colour. Colours placed opposite each other on the colour wheel – for instance, red and green – are called complementary or contrasting colours.

Then there are the monochromatic colours, split complementaries, and related (analogous) colours. Do not be put off by these technical terms, because they are easily understood.

Thus, monochromatic colours are those that describe the various hues, tones and shades of the same colour family – for example, red passing through to pink. A split complementary uses a main colour and two adjacent colours to its complement: thus blue's split complementaries would be yellow-orange and red-orange.

Related (analogous) shades can be any three to five shades, tints or tones of colours: thus blue would bring blue-violet, violet, red-violet, red.

While not an essential item for dyeing, a good colour wheel does make colour more understandable. Those illustrated are extremely helpful, and give a better understanding of the various terms used in the preceding paragraphs. There is also a black and white 'Create-a-Colour Wheel', a 'hands-on' tool which teaches you how to mix colours by helping you to understand colour relationships. Many teachers of dyeing encourage their students to make their own colour wheels to enhance their understanding of how colours work. There are also many good books on the use of colour.

DYEING FABRICS AND YARNS

Dyeing fabrics and yarns is part of the fun of rug making. All fibres, both traditional and non-traditional, have a texture, and these textures are often enhanced by the use of colour. Dyeing your own materials adds another dimension to the satisfaction with your work. Fabric paints can also be used on the background, and on the fabrics to be used for rug making; a variety of manufacturers provide these paints, and their instructions should be followed.

Our ancestors had to use natural plant dyes to dye their fabrics for rug making; however, collecting the plants and preparing them was, and is, very time-consuming, and sometimes the basic ingredients are quite difficult to obtain. Nevertheless, as a result of the growing modern-day interest in natural dyeing, many more suppliers

Opposite: Two results of plaited dyeing.

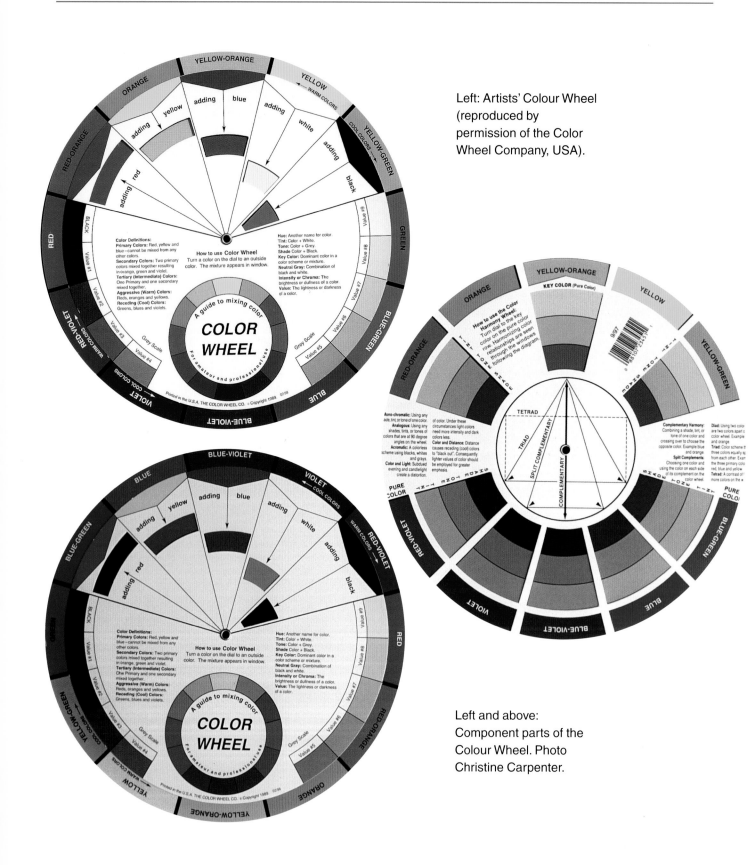

Left: Artists' Colour Wheel (reproduced by permission of the Color Wheel Company, USA).

Left and above: Component parts of the Colour Wheel. Photo Christine Carpenter.

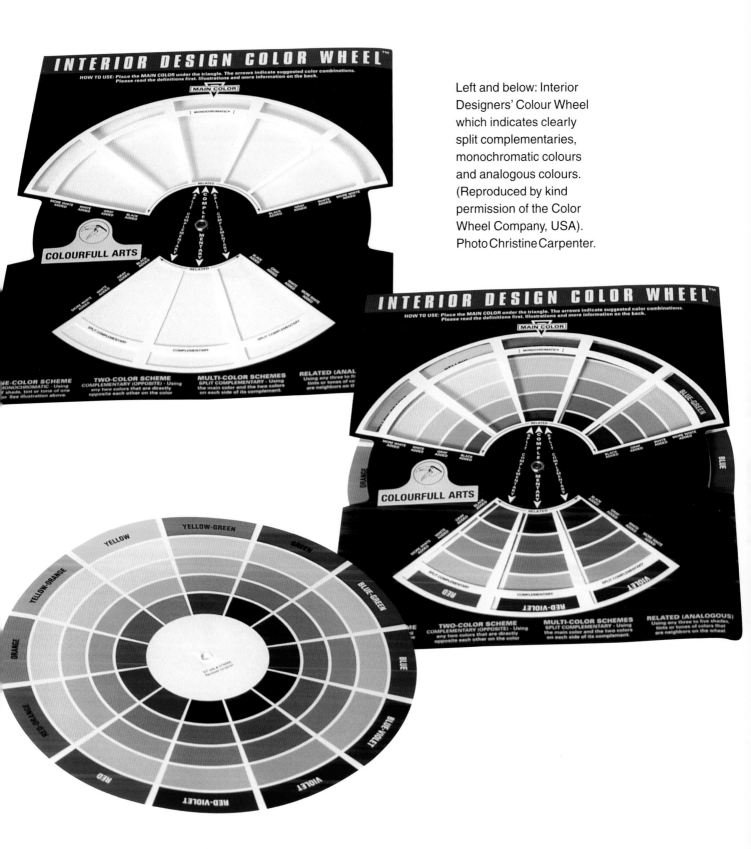

Left and below: Interior Designers' Colour Wheel which indicates clearly split complementaries, monochromatic colours and analogous colours. (Reproduced by kind permission of the Color Wheel Company, USA). Photo Christine Carpenter.

are listing dried natural ingredients in their catalogues.

Chemical dyes are produced from synthetic compounds. The history of dyeing is a long story and is one which can be researched elsewhere.

The two basic chemical dyes which are relevant to our purposes are known as fibre-reactive and acid dyes: fibre-reactive dyes work best on cotton, silk, linen and viscose rayon; acid dyes are suitable for wool, silk, synthetic fibres, mohair and cashmere. Fibre-reactive dyes can be used with wool, but the results are usually considerably paler. Although there are other types of dye, these two are most suitable for rag rug making.

In North America, Cushing acid dyes are widely used by rag rug makers, and are available in an extensive range of colours.

There are various suppliers of powdered dyes, and they are listed at the back of the book. Small tins of prepared commercial dyes are expensive and have to be used up immediately. It is more economic to buy your dye in small packets or jars and to make up the dye solution yourself; by doing this you can keep them, properly sealed and in a cool place, for up to one year. After that time the colour starts to deteriorate, although the dye is still usable. You will find that there isn't the extensive range of colours available compared with commercial household dyes, but you can have great fun mixing the colours yourself.

Safety First

Before you begin a dyeing session there are some basic safety guidelines to observe:

1. Most people use their kitchen for dyeing purposes: if this is what you do, be sure to remove all utensils and foodstuffs from the area in which you are going to work.

2. It is advisable to drape plastic sheeting over all work surfaces; the sort used to protect furniture when decorating is ideal. You may have to anchor it to the work surface with a few weights. One useful tip: lay newspaper on top of the plastic on the work surface to absorb any spillage of water or dye.

3. A well ventilated room is essential; so is the availability of water.

4. Keep any equipment you use for dyeing for that purpose only.

5. All my dye bottles and equipment are kept in large plastic storage boxes, and they are stored away from other kitchen equipment.

6. Always protect your hands by wearing strong rubber gloves.

7. A protective apron or overall is advisable; also wear clothes that you do not mind being splashed with dye.

8. When handling dry dye powder every supplier advises wearing a face mask as a precaution against inhaling it.

You will find that most of the equipment for dyeing is already available in your home. However, anything you use for dyeing must not be used for any other purpose.

Dyeing in the Microwave Oven

Microwave dyeing is great fun and wonderful results can be achieved,

though be aware that it is not suitable for larger amounts of fabric; I would advise handling no more than 8oz dry weight at a time. Skeins of yarn can also be dyed in the microwave oven.

Besides the oven itself you will need: plastic and/or Pyrex dishes which are microwave-proof, polythene tissue, a spray bottle such as the kind you use for spraying indoor plants, rubber gloves, and small rollers – the latter obtainable from artists' suppliers. The rollers are optional, as you can use the pressure of your fingers, but I find that rollers work the dye into the material more efficiently. Oven gloves and tongs are also useful when taking hot dishes from the microwave, and materials out of the dishes.

For accurate dyeing you will need measuring and weighing equipment to measure dye powders and fabrics: a set of measuring spoons ranging from ¼ teaspoon to 1 tablespoon, and some scales for weighing fabrics and dyes are recommended. In some cases you need to weigh out 5g which can be difficult to do on household scales. As a rough guide, 5g is one rounded 5ml plastic spoon, and anything greater can be measured by using a 50ml plastic medicine measure: thus 10g = the 10ml mark, 25g = the 25ml mark and 50g = the 50ml mark. If you are considering doing a lot of dyeing it saves time to make up 10g of dye power.

Make sure that you always clean your microwave oven extremely thoroughly after you have used it for dyeing purposes, for obvious reasons.

Above: Dyeing equipment: plastic dish, polythene tissue, rubber gloves, small rollers. Photo Christine Carpenter.

Right: Face mask,
measuring spoons.

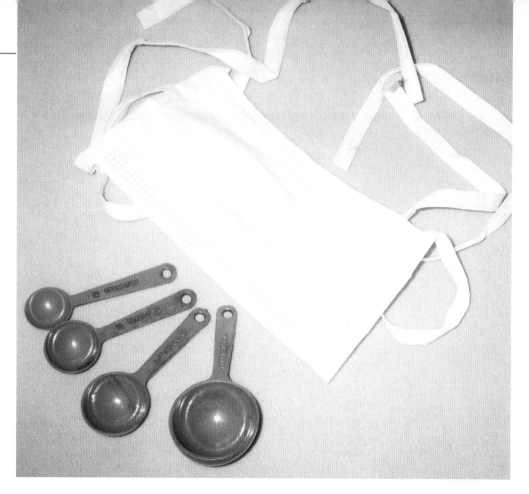

Notes on Dyeing

Mix up your dyes according to the instructions supplied by the distributor. Basically dye powder is dissolved in a small amount of tepid water to make a smooth paste and is then made up to 100ml by the addition of boiling water; this is called your stock solution. However, formulas do differ from one supplier to another, so follow the instructions provided.

Keep a selection of bottles in which to store your dyes. Plastic bottles are lighter than glass and are safer, but glass bottles have a longer life. Always label your containers with the colour and make of the dye, the percentage solution, and the date on which it was made up.

It is helpful to keep notes that you can refer to on what you do, the fabric you use, the amount of dye and the method of dyeing used.

Preparing your Fabric for Dyeing

Always wash your fabrics to remove any dressing or dry cleaning compound. If using old clothes, remove all the hems, seams, selvages and zips, and it is helpful to felt knitwear items – if this isn't already the reason for their being relegated to rag rug use – otherwise they might disintegrate when cut into strips. Wash them in a 60-degree wash cycle of your washing machine using ordinary detergent, and they will felt enough to use without disintegrating, but without also going thick and 'boarded'.

If you are using new fabrics wash them, and then cut or tear them into manageable pieces. When washing torn fabrics in your washing machine it is advisable to put them into bags used for washing delicate items, or in a pillowcase fastened with safety pins;

this way any loose fibres will not clog your machine.

You can do all this preparation before you actually use the fabric, and either dry everything and use it another time, or go straight on to the dyeing preparation.

The Dyeing Procedure

Your fabric should be soaked in a bath or bucket for at least an hour before dyeing, and preferably overnight. Prepare a bowl or bucket with 1 litre of warm water to which has been added 50ml of white vinegar and a drop of liquid detergent. If you have a lot of fabric you wish to dye, increase the quantities accordingly: thus 2 litres to 100ml of vinegar, and so on.

When using dyes in conjunction with microwave dyeing I decant undiluted solutions into small squeegee bottles (the kind used by hairdressers to dispense a perm or colour solution are best), or used yoghurt containers. There are also soft drink bottles commonly seen on the supermarket shelves which have a small protrusion on the bottle top so you can drink without actually opening the bottle: these are ideal for holding and dispensing dyes, although the

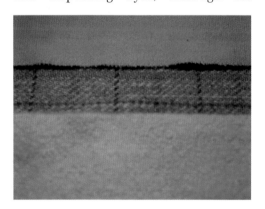

Component parts of plait – cream blanket, wool tweed, wool and cotton mixture.

squeegee bottles are better for dispensing small amounts of dye. Dyes can be used as they are, or different coloured dyes can be mixed together, or they can be diluted, or grey or black can be added, or a small amount of water – though be careful you do not dilute the dye too much. Also, when dyeing fabric and yarns, bear in mind the fact that colours look much brighter when the material is wet; they will dry to a lighter shade.Good dyeing is when the dye goes right into the material, and you can ensure this happens by using finger pressure or rollers. (The exception to this is when ball dyeing, see later.)

Colour can also be simmered out of some materials, mainly wool and cotton. This is often achieved by long gentle simmering, or simmering in water to which a few drops of household ammonia have been added, or using a proprietary powder that acts as a powerful remover of colour. If using the latter do be very careful not to simmer for too long as it draws the colour from the cloth very quickly.

MICROWAVE DYEING RECIPES

Dyeing a Plait

Three strips of material are needed for this, and fabrics that I would suggest might be suitable are a cream or white wool, a tweed or check material, and another material (possibly a wool together with other fibres) which might be cream or a pastel colour. The materials take up the dye in different ways, but make sure that they all have the same colourway.

1.   Cut each piece of your material (always on the straight) about 3ft (1m) in length and about 5in wide.
Fasten the strips together at one end by

Above: Plait caught together with rubber bands, ready for dyeing.

tissue: this should be long enough to take all of the plait plus a couple of inches. The roll is perforated, but ignore the perforations.

8. Remove the plait from soaking and squeeze it out gently; don't wring it out because, although the fabric shouldn't be dripping, it still needs to be quite wet. Lay it on the polythene tissue.

wrapping them round with a piece of string or rubber bands, or by stitching them. Never fasten them with metal items such as safety pins, as it is dangerous to use metal in a microwave oven.

2. Loosely plait the strips together and tie or stitch the other end.

3. Put the plait (or plaits) to soak in the warm water and white vinegar solution (the proportions are given on the previous page) for at least an hour, but overnight is preferable.

4. About three different dye colours work well, but this is a matter of personal choice.

5. Take your dye from the stock solutions and decant them into small beakers or squeegee bottles (about 100ml of each). If you want paler colours dilute your stock solution by mixing 25ml of dye with 25ml of water. If you want it even paler then put 10ml of dye with about 40ml of water, but be careful not to over-dilute.

6. Make up a mix of two parts water to one part white vinegar, and put it in your spray bottle.

7. On top of your thick wad of newspaper lay out your polythene

9. Take your squeegee bottle or container and dribble one of the dyes down the complete length of the plait; work it in using either a roller or finger pressure, making sure that it really enters the material. Repeat this with the other two colours. You may wish to turn the plait over onto its side to work the other colours in – it is up to you. The plait shouldn't dry out, if it feels dry then spray it with the water and vinegar mix.

10. When you feel satisfied that the dye has penetrated the fabric, tuck the ends of the tissue over the ends of the plait and then roll the rest up round the plait, making a parcel. Make sure the tissue completely encloses it because if any fabric is left showing it will be damaged by the heat of the microwave oven.

11. Put some water into the microwave dish you are going to use, just enough to cover the base. If the plait is too big to put flat in the microwave dish, coil it round to fit.

12. If you don't have a turntable on your microwave oven, make sure you turn the container half way through cooking. Also at the half-way stage I recommend letting the fabric rest in the oven for about a minute, before going on to the final few minutes.

13.   Set your microwave oven to about 700/750. Some ovens have just a low, medium and high setting, in which case set it to high. Cook for about six to eight minutes. Take the parcel of fabric out of the microwave, using oven gloves and tongs, and put it, still covered with the tissue, onto a wad of newspaper and allow it to cool. The dyeing process continues while the material is cooling so it is important that you allow this to happen.

14.   When the parcel has completely cooled down, unwrap it and wash it under tepid water. Gently squeeze out the excess water; alternatively you could put it in a salad spinner and spin it as fast as you can. Then hang it up to dry.

If you don't have a microwave oven you can steam your parcel for 15 – 20 minutes: prepare your fabric as for microwave dyeing, then place it in a colander and put this over a saucepan of hot water; cover the colander with a lid. The fabric should not come into contact with the hot water. Again, allow it to cool before rinsing.

Salt Cellar Dyeing

I am indebted to Marion Ham and Gail Horton of the USA for this recipe. This is a very random, hit-and-miss dyeing procedure which produces a speckled effect. You will need at least three glass salt cellars (you can generally pick these up really cheaply in charity (thrift) shops) – it is easier to wash out any residual dye from glass ones than it is from plastic, for example. After washing upend them on a wire tray to dry thoroughly. Use a face mask when using dry dye powder.

1.   Pre-soak your piece of material in the water and white vinegar solution described above. A piece of fabric measuring 10 x 18in is a convenient size to work with.

2.   Place your tissue on your work surface; you may have to overlap two pieces for width. Make sure there is enough tissue at each end to tuck over the ends of the material.

3.   Put dye powder into each of the salt cellars – about a quarter of a teaspoon of dry dye for each cellar is a workable amount.

4.   Take the material from the bowl or bucket and let it drain, or squeeze out the surplus water. Sprinkle each dye over the material until dots of dye cover the wool.

5.   Tuck in the ends of the tissue, and then roll up the material and tissue together like a Swiss roll. You can do several pieces at the same time. Then place them in a microwave container to which has been added about 1in of water.

6.   Cook for 6min on 750/high, and then follow the same process as for the plait.
Alternatively you can steam the material, as in the previous recipe.

Dyeing in a Ball

Cut your woollen material into strips about 2 x 80in (maximum). You will need a reasonably high-sided microwave dish for this, and also the largest size that will fit into your microwave oven without jamming on the sides. Depending on the size of your container you can dye several balls at the same time, but they must be in a single layer in the microwave dish.

1.   Loosely roll the strips into a ball, tucking in the ends so that they do not unravel.

Above: Salt cellar dyeing.

2.   Soak the balls in warm water and white vinegar, as before, together with a tiny squirt of washing-up liquid.

3.   Decide what colours you want to work with; two or three work well as they blend into the wool, but obviously it is your choice.

4.   Take your stock dye solution and put about 1in of the first dye colour into your microwave dish.

5.   Take your woollen balls of material from soak, and gently squeeze out the excess water. Put your fabric into the dish and cover it completely with tissue. Don't have any fabric exposed to the microwave oven or it will crisp.

6.   Cook for about 6 – 8 minutes on 750/high.

7.   Carefully remove the dish from the microwave oven, using oven gloves as it will all be very hot. Gently take the balls from the dish, using tongs, and put them into the sink, or into another heatproof receptacle. They should have absorbed most of the dye, but if there is any left, pour it away.

8.   Pour some of the second dye solution into the dish until it is 1in deep and return the balls to the dish with an undyed portion facing downwards into the dye. Be careful when handling the balls as they will still be hot.

9.   Repeat the instructions as for the first application for as many times as you choose.

When you have finished the final dyeing, place the balls on a clean wad of paper towels or newspaper and let them cool down, then wash them out in warm water. Squeeze out the excess moisture, or use a salad spinner, and hang the strips up to dry.

This process is not suitable for use with the steaming method.

Random Dyeing

Random dyeing is fun, but the effects cannot be replicated: it is just a fun way to use up any dye left over after other dyeing procedures. Prepare your material as given in other 'recipes', using up to 8oz dry weight of material.

1.   Place the gently squeezed material onto your tissue. Take up your dyes (again, three is a good number) in their squeegee bottles, and dribble them over your fabric in whatever pattern you wish, or just randomly. Work the dye well into the fabric, using either your fingers or a roller so that the dye goes

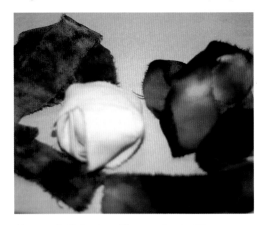

Above: Ball dyeing. The centre ball is undyed. Two dyed balls using different colourways.

through to the other side of the fabric.

2.   Roll up your material into a Swiss roll, as described earlier, and put it into your microwave dish plus water. Place this in the microwave oven, and cook for the usual time.

3.   Allow to cool, and then rinse out in warm water.

The steaming method can be used for this technique.

FABRIC PAINTING

If you have a lot of sunset, seascape or whatever, dye a long strip and then cut it up into microwave-manageable pieces. It is preferable to use white or cream fabric.

If you are using a long strip of fabric (remember, when you hook, your strip usually covers about a third of the area) cut enough tissue to wrap up all the strip plus allowing overlap for each piece.

All the usual directions apply:

1.   Put the dyes into containers large enough to take the paintbrush; plastic cups are ideal, or washed yoghurt pots.

2.   If you want a skyscape, decide on the colours you want to work with; for instance for a stormy sky you might want grey, blues and reds. Dilute some dyes, or add black or grey for tones.

3.   When the dyes are prepared, try them out on cheap white lining paper first, and then you will have an idea of what the effect will be before launching out onto the fabric. This way you can see whether the dyes are the chosen colour, or whether you need to add a drop of another colour or more water.

4.   When you are satisfied, paint the dyes onto the fabric with the paintbrush, working them firmly into the fabric. Do not have straight lines, but overlap your colours – use your spray bottle to make the colours run into one another. Use your imagination!

The techniques can be used for landscapes, seascapes, gardens – the list is endless. You will never be able to repeat the sequence exactly, but be careful to keep records of the ways in which you mixed the dyes, or diluted them, as you will find it helpful if you want to reproduce something similar at a later date.

There are many other ideas that will occur to you: experiment – you will have failures and successes, but you will learn from your efforts. I have used mainly woollen materials, but the ideas can be adapted to other fabrics. If you have any doubts about a fabric's suitability for microwave dyeing, try a small amount and see what happens.

Fabrics must always be protected by a plastic film or lid or they will frizzle when microwaved, and could be in danger of catching fire.

I always press my dry material strips after dyeing: somehow it seems to make them look more interesting.

Yarns can also be dyed in the microwave in the same way as woollen, silk and cotton fabrics.

Above: Squeegee bottles, plastic containers and a 1in brush for landscape dyeing.

Above: Results of landscape dyeing.

3 Hooky and Proddy

HOOKING

This is without doubt by far my favourite technique, because it is so versatile. You can use it on its own, or in conjunction with other textile techniques.

Basically a portion of a long strip of material is pulled by a tool with an acute angled hook from the reverse side of a base fabric through to the right side, thereby producing a loop. Three sizes of hook are illustrated here: the larger one is for working with woollen and other similar weights of fabric or yarn, the medium one for finer cuts, and the very fine hook is for extremely thin strips of fabric, and in particular yarn; there is a knack in using the very fine hook as it does not have the shaped shank of the other two hooks. When withdrawing the hook up through the base fabric, just press it lightly against the lower thread, thus enlarging the hole enough to avoid catching the hook on the upper thread. When using the fine hook and fine yarn or fine cut material, work into nearly every hole. Very delicate shadings of colour can be achieved.

You may find it easier to work on a frame (see Chapter 2).

Preparing the Base Fabric

First prepare your base fabric (page 15). Measure out what you need, bearing in mind it must be 3in larger all round than the diameter of the finished rug.

If using the circular frame, cut the piece of base fabric about 5 to 6in larger all round than the size you want the finished piece to be.

In all cases sew zig-zag stitches around the edges of the base fabric to prevent fraying.

If you have a complicated design, put it onto the base fabric before you attach this to the frame. First mark out the size of the finished rug; the design can then be drawn out free-hand, or transferred

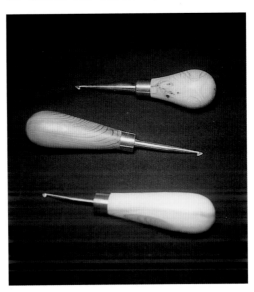

Left: Modern hooks.

Opposite: Silk randomly dyed for use with the silk painting panel.(Mary Day Silk Painting Studio)

using a transfer pen and tracing paper or a heavy grease crayon and tracing paper (transfer pens can generally be obtained from good haberdashery or needlecraft stores). Using the tracing paper, draw over the design with the pen, then turn the paper face down onto the base fabric with the transfer design facing onto the fabric, and iron it on with a hot iron, using a pressing, rather than an ironing movement. If using grey polyester, use a lower heat setting or the heat might

damage the polyester. The grease crayon will not give such a clear line after ironing onto the base fabric, and you may have to go over the outlines with a waterproof felt-tip pen. If transferring lettering, bear in mind that the lettering will be reversed.

Preparing to Work with a Frame

Fix the base fabric onto the frame using a staple gun and staples. If you do not have a staple gun you can use drawing pins (thumb tacks), but they do have a tendency to jump out during the course of working the rug. Be generous with your staples and put them in horizontally to the edge of the frame. Staple along one length and one width in an L shape, making sure the staples are close together. Then fix the other two sides, pulling the fabric taut and keeping its threads as square to the frame as you can. Pay particular attention to the corners by stapling right into them. The front of the work is the side where the staples are.

If using the circular frame, put your design onto your base fabric before stretching it over the inside ring, then place the outside ring over the inside ring. Keeping the fabric tightly stretched over the inside ring, tighten up the screw on the outside ring, and keep turning the screw until the fabric is held very tautly. Lessen the tension when you are not working on the piece of work; this will prevent the loops being flattened.

If using the frame with dowels or the Lowery frame, put your design on the base fabric before stretching it on the frame. Follow the manufacturer's instructions for framing up your base material.

With most frames you will find you cannot work up to the inside edge of the frame, and so you will need to mark the diameter of your work. Do this by drawing a border about ½in (12mm) in from the inside edge of the frame: place a sharp, soft pencil between two threads of the fabric, then pull it down towards you, keeping it between the same two threads all the way. Turn your frame and do the same on the other three sides. This ensures that you have a straight edge to work against, even if you have distorted the fabric when you stretched it on the frame.

These instructions also apply if you are using a picture frame.

In the case of the hoop, or with frames where you have to roll the fabric on, mark the diameter of your work and put on the completed design before you put it on the frame. Always try and keep the threads of the base fabric parallel to the frame when putting the design onto the hessian.

Preparing the Hooking Materials

If possible, wash the fabrics you are going to work with before using them.

Then cut some of your selected material into strips about ¼ to ⅜in (6–10cm) wide, and always on the straight – never cut them on the bias unless you are using a twill weave fabric. The length of your strip can be anything from 6in (150 cm) upwards. Initially cut just a few strips, because unless you have tried them out on a

sample frame, you may find that you do not like the effect they give.

If you use a rotary cutter and mat ensure that you have a straight edge of fabric to cut against. Align the straight edge of the fabric against a line on the grid of the cutting mat. Place the metal edge of the ruler the required distance from the edge of the material and, pushing the cutter away from you, cut along the side of the ruler. If using the 'Shape Cut', follow the manufacturer's instructions.

Remember to cover the blade of your rotary cutter with the guard as soon as you have finished using it.

If using scissors, try to cut your strips as straight along the grain as you can. Some materials can be torn, especially wool and cotton.

The Hooking Technique

You are now ready to begin. Hold the hook in your right hand with it nestling comfortably between your thumb and forefinger (if you are left-handed,

Left: Dragging a pencil down through two threads of hessian to establish a straight line. Photo Christine Carpenter.

Top right: Holding hook
and pushing into the
base fabric. Photo
Christine Carpenter.

reverse the following instructions):

1.   Take the strip of material you
are going to use, and hold one end
loosely between the thumb and
forefinger of your left hand. Position
the hand holding the strip under the
frame at exactly the point where your
hook will enter.

2.   Hold the hook slightly at an angle
and push it firmly into the base fabric
from the front (where the design is) to
the reverse side. Don't be too gentle – the
bigger the hole, the easier it is to bring
your material back through to the
front. And don't worry about the hole
being too big, because when you make
the next hole, the threads displaced
by the previous hole will close up
automatically, thus gripping the loops of
material firmly into the base fabric.

3.   Catch the end of the fabric strip
with your hook. Pull the hook and the
strip end up to the front of your base
fabric, about 1in (25cm) above the
surface. If by mistake you pull through
more of the strip than you intended,
just gently pull it back until the
requisite 1in (25cm) is showing above
the fabric. All your ends, both starting
and finishing, are brought up to the
front of your work. By doing this you
ensure that, when pushing the hook
into the base fabric, it cannot catch on
any loose ends and pull out previously
made loops.

4.   Working from right to left, move
your hook about two threads away, and
then push it firmly into the base fabric at
an angle as before. Hold the strip of
material loosely between the thumb and
forefinger of your left hand and just
above where the hook will be pushed in.
Let the hook find the material, and pull a
loop to the front to a height of about

Top right: Holding hook and pushing into the base fabric. Photo Christine Carpenter.

Middle right: Bringing up
one end of the material to
the front of the work. Photo
Christine Carpenter.

Bottom right: Hooking up
the next loop. Photo
Christine Carpenter.

½in (12mm). It's a strange thing, but
everyone finds their own level of loop:
some like to hook high and others lower.
Your loops should be close enough
together so that no hessian is visible

curves, as the loops meld in better. You do not have to work across from one edge to another.

TROUBLESHOOTING

You will know if you are hooking correctly by checking the reverse of your work: you should see something similar to a smooth running stitch. If there are lumps on the back then you are not making the holes big enough and the material cannot pull back easily through the base hessian.

If you find you are pulling out the previous loop you have made, then you are holding the strip of material too tightly between your thumb and forefinger. You should always let it run loosely.

When you come to the end of the strip of material, pull the end up to the front of the work. Never leave ends dangling at the back, nor be tempted to run a strip

Left: Reverse of work showing material held loosely between finger and thumb and the hook getting right under the strip. Photo Christine Carpenter.

between them, but not so tightly packed that it causes the base hessian to 'hump'.

5.   Work from right to left (if you are left-handed reverse the instructions), repeating the hook, scoop, loop sequence. Unless you want a definitive straight line it is better to work in slight

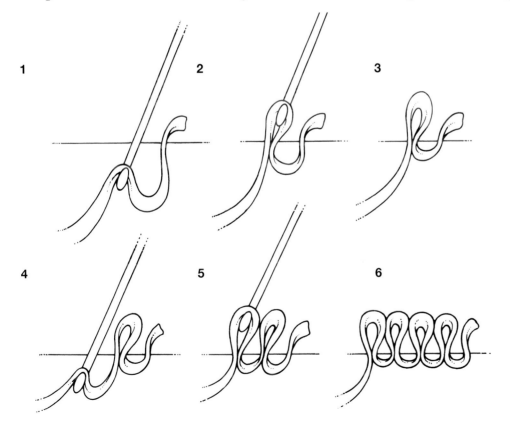

Left: Sketch showing the hooking process.

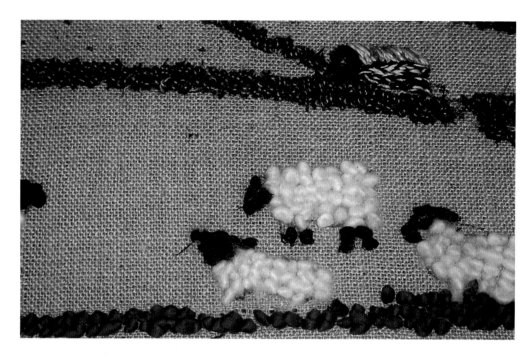

Right: Work in progress showing the higher hooked outlines. The sheep are hooked using actual fleece.

Right: Ann Davies, Kaleidoscope, 1986. Hooked rug with woollen and cotton materials. (28 x 36in)

from one area to another. If you do, your hook might catch on the strip and you could pull out previous loops. It is a simple matter to bring the material up to the front, clip it off level with the rest of your loops, and start again.

When you have finished a strip of material and have brought its end up to the front, go back into the same hole and bring up the loose end of the next strip; this ensures that there is a double thickness of material similar to the thickness of the loop. However, don't worry if you cannot make joins in this way – it isn't always possible.

When commencing a row of loops above or below the first row, always leave the same gap between them as you have between the loops – for example, two threads between each loop, two threads between each row.

When using the fine hook, a slightly different technique is used. You would also use finer mesh base material such as an even-weave fabric or linen. As the shank of the hook is not shaped as the other two hooks are, when pulling the hook back through the base fabric put a little pressure against the weave by pressing the shank of the hook against the weave, thus enlarging the hole and enabling the hook to come out easily without snagging on the mesh of the weave.

You can start your work in the centre and move out, or vice versa. Use your hook as a paintbrush. The only exception is when doing any outlining which entails the use of a single line of fabric. In order to keep this visible when hooking the main body of work, hook it first, and slightly higher than the rest of the pile.

To avoid being left with a lot of background to complete the work, do some of the pattern and some of the background.

Before taking your completed work from the frame, turn it over and look at the reverse: you may well find small gaps showing, even though the front looks solidly packed. Take some wooden toothpicks (they stay in the hessian better than plastic ones) and insert them from the reverse to the front. Then turn your work to the front and hook into the areas marked by the toothpicks, trying not to pack the loops too tightly.

When you are satisfied with your work, cut all the loose ends level with the pile of your loops, if you have not already cut the ends off as you worked.

FINISHING OFF

Remove your work from the frame. If removing staples, a flat staple remover, an old screwdriver or a knife work better than the claw type of staple remover. Brush lightly over the pile with a clothes brush to remove any excess fluff.

Next, press the rug. Lay it, pile side down, onto a blanket or large towel. Then take a damp cloth and place it over the back of the rug, and press it by using a gentle stamping motion, rather than a gliding one. When you have finished, turn the rug so that the loops are the right way up, and allow it to dry naturally. Keep the rug flat while it dries.

This method of pressing only applies to rugs and other articles where the heat will not harm the materials used. Do not use it on work containing plastic or anything that is likely to melt. Finishing is covered more fully in Chapter 5.

Some Variations

Now let us look at some variations. They may not be entirely suitable for rugs but they are ideal for wall hangings, cushions and so on, and if used in conjunction with various other textile techniques, can produce very exciting results.

REVERSE HOOKING

In this technique the running stitch which is normally on the reverse of the rug appears on the front. As you will see in the sample illustrated, the leaf appears in relief. This effect was obtained in the following way:

1.   The leaf was hooked first using the normal method, then the work was turned over and marked out in a grid on the reverse side, using the dragged pencil method described earlier. If you are using a thickish material your grid will need to be wider than if you are using a more finely cut strip.

2.   Mark out your grid with each line going vertically, equidistant from the next, then cross your lines horizontally using the same measurements; the base fabric will end up looking like squared paper.

3.   Working with the base fabric grid side up, insert your hook and pull up an end at the edge of the grid. Then proceed, bringing up a loop at the intersection of every square, and continue across the whole work. On the front you will see the running stitch which normally appears on the reverse. Each row should touch the previous one so that you do not see any hessian between the rows. More than one colour can be used, or you can make a brick effect by hooking every other row between the previous row with a similar or contrasting fabric and with the loop placed between the running stitches.

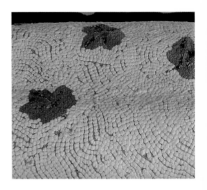

Above: What the back of a piece of hooking looks like. Photo Christine Carpenter.

Top right: Leaf hooked,
background reverse
hooking.

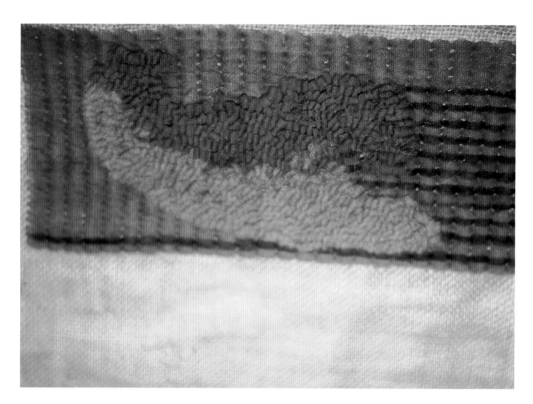

Bottom right: Showing
how the reverse hooking
is done.

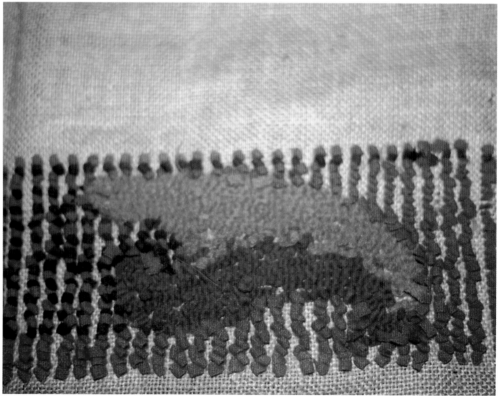

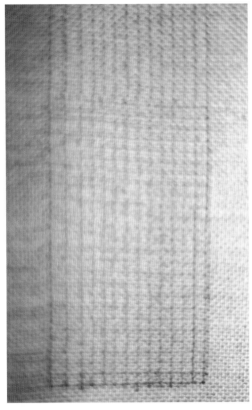

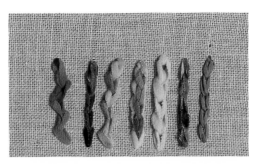

Top left: Grid marked out with the dragged pencil method.

Top right: Chain stitch using the hook, and variations.

Bottom right: Flowers. Centre close hooking. Clockwise: yellow blanket, stretch velvet, dyed net, organza.

material underneath the base hessian, and bring a fairly large loop up to the front, holding the two ends with your fingers underneath the work.

2.   Insert the hook at the end of this loop, away from the start, and bring up another loop. Continue in this way until the whole strip is formed into loops.

3.   Bring the end of the strip up through the last loop, turn your work over, push the hook from the reverse side to the right side just beyond the last loop, catch the strip and bring it back to beneath the hessian. Cut off the end of the strip and catch with a dab of glue or a stitch. The loops can be built up one on top of another to form a dense texture. This method would not be entirely practical for rugs, but it gives an interesting texture for wall hangings, for example.

Bottom left: Brick effect using reverse hooking.

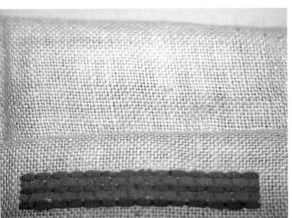

CHAIN STITCH

This can add texture to your work. You will need to cut a long strip of fabric.

1.   Working with the right side up as for normal hooking, hold a strip of

FLOWERS

1.   Make a centre with normal length loops, working round and round. Bring

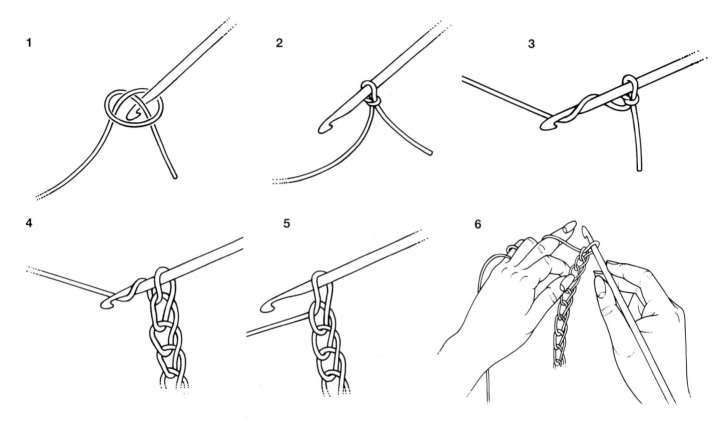

1 **2** **3**

4 **5** **6**

Above: Sketch of how to work single crochet.

Opposite: Selection of hand-made silk paper. (the paper shed)

your end up into the loops and lose it in the pile.

2.   Take up a long strip of material, and make long loops round the centre loops; they can be fine, or big and chunky. Leave the end at the back of the work and either stitch it or stick it down with a dab of fabric glue.

3.   If you want the loops made on the front of the work to lie really flat you can stitch them down. Use a fine thread so that it doesn't show.

USING SINGLE CROCHET

Sometimes a yarn is too thin to be hooked on its own, but used in a length of single crochet, the effect is a texture within a texture. Single crochet is easy to do: using either a crochet hook or the hooking tool, start by making a slip loop about 6in (15cm) from the end of the thread.

1.   To make a slip loop, hold the thread between the thumb and forefinger of the left hand, and with the right hand, form it into a loop; the left hand holds it in place.

2.   Take up the hook in your right hand, and as if using a pencil, insert it through the loop and under the thread. Draw a loop through, but do not remove it from the hook. Pull the thread to bring the loop close to the hook, but not too tightly.

3.   With the palm of the hand facing down, hold the knot and the short end of the thread between the thumb and the forefinger of the left hand. Pass the working thread over the back of the fingers, under the 'ring' finger and round the little finger. The thread should lie firmly but not too tightly; getting the tension right may seem difficult to master at first, but it comes with

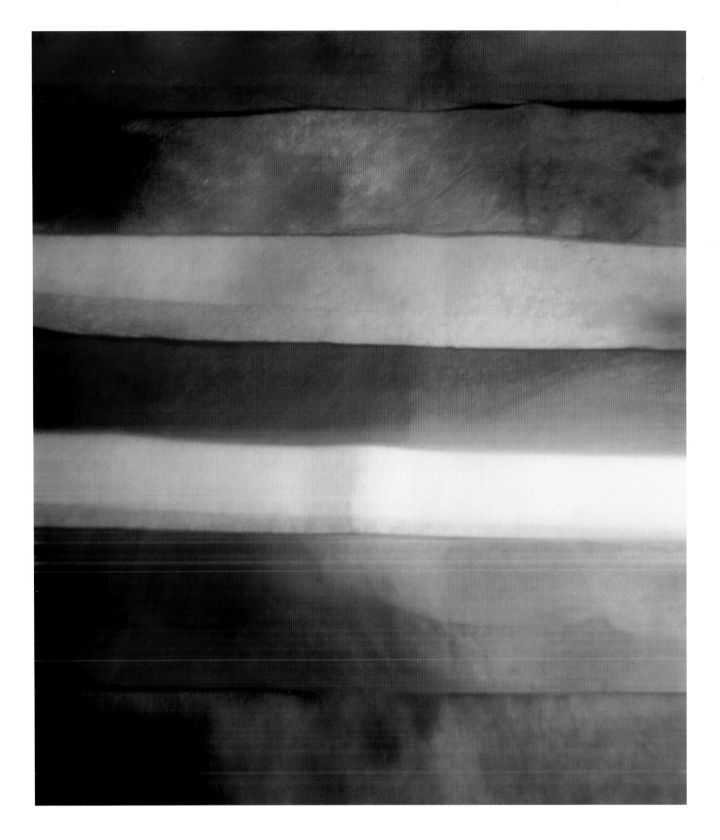

Wooden box covered with hand-made paper, with a simple hooked area on the lid. hooking worked on fine linen mesh, using strips of tissue paper. (Ann Davies)

Below: Single crochet hooked. This produces a texture within a texture. Photo Christine Carpenter.

practice. Different people hold their thread in different ways, but the main thing is to be able to control the thread comfortably.

4.   Raise the second finger to make a working space between the first two fingers. Pass the hook under the yarn and catch the yarn with the hook. Draw the thread through the loop on the hook. This produces one chain. Repeat this until the chain is the length you require.

SILK PAPER

Although unsuitable for anything that will wear, silk paper has possibilities. The box illustrated has had silk paper applied to the top and sides, and the lid has been worked using strips of silk paper cut to about 1in wide, and hooked on a fine linen mesh – hessian is too abrasive for this fine paper.

OTHER SUGGESTIONS

In his book *Rare Hooked Rugs*, William Winthrop Kent gives two variations. In

his preface he kindly writes '...any material herein may be reproduced if due credit is given. This is asked that others may learn of the book and its helpfulness (if any) be extended'. In view of this permission the piece entitled 'A Hooked Rug with Variations' is reproduced in its entirety. (NB: In North America hessian is called burlap.)

A HOOKED RUG WITH VARIATIONS

'Clair Green once wrote in *The Rural New Yorker* of an original way of making a hooked fabric which she and that paper permit me to quote:

I had finished reseating a chair, and needed something for a protective covering. Being in a mood for mild adventure, I took my rug hook, a piece of clean, new burlap with some choice soft rags, and sat down to see what I could do with them. I know some will think this too mild an adventure to hold interest, but I am sure many will understand my satisfaction when presently there appeared on the burlap a combination of loops that held definite promise of beauty and utility. This effort gave rise to another idea which works out into an unusually nice rug and is rather quicker to do than the regular hooking. Both of these styles are illustrated and described herewith, and I hope will give others as much pleasure in the making as I have had.

I seldom use a frame for rugs, chiefly because I keep my rug making for pick-up work and dislike the cumber-someness of a frame – although one does facilitate the hooking. In a previous article, I have described the arrangement of the burlap over an old-fashioned towel rack, and this is very satisfactory for general purposes.

To make the first as illustrated: Begin about 1½ inches from the edge of the burlap in the upper left-hand corner and draw up a row of loops three-quarters to

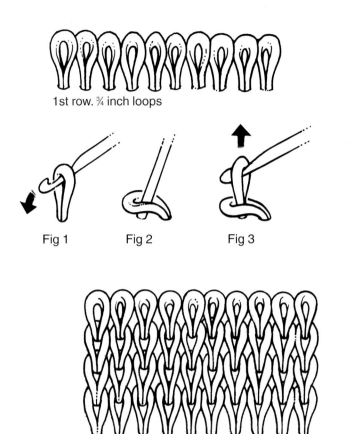

1st row. ¾ inch loops

Fig 1   Fig 2   Fig 3

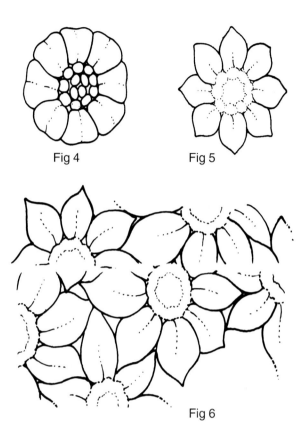

Fig 4   Fig 5

Fig 6

an inch long, following the line of the fabric and extending all the way across the width. It is important that these loops be uniform in height. For the second row, proceed as shown in Figs. 1, 2 and 3, putting the hook through the loop of the first row. Skip five or six strands of burlap, thus drawing the loop out to its full length and inserting hook at a point directly below the upper loop, draw another loop up through the first. Repeat along the entire row, then work the third and remaining rows in the same manner, being careful to draw out each loop but not stretching it to curl the foundation.

I am confident that it will be possible to develop this method in a great many more ways than I have attempted, both as to colouring and patterns. I have tried the striped and shaded effects, and next intend to work out an Indian design on a plain background.

Figs. 4, 5, 6 and 7 show the style that I call the 'lazy daisy' – although the flowers really resemble single Dahlias – and is the one I used for chair seat. This is my 'pet', and can be adapted to a number of uses beside rugs, and be developed in colour combinations that are charming and delightful. It is one of those things that challenge one's imagination and ingenuity, and amply repays every bit of care and thought given to it.

Leave an inch and a half margin on all edges for hemming. Decide first on the width of flower wanted; 2½ to 3 inches is a good size for most purposes, and I shall

Above: William Winthrop Kent, *Rare Hooked Rugs*.

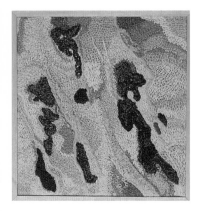

Above: Seascape: Panel showing hooking, wrapped chenille and embroidery. (Ann Davies)

Right: Unicorn hooked using lurex fabrics. Background even-weave curtain material. (Ann Davies)

Silk painting ready for central panel. (Christina Davison). (Mary Day Silk Painting Studios).

Random- dyed silk ready for hooking round the silk central panel. (Mary Day Silk Painting Studios).

use that width in this description. Choose a strip of soft cloth cut a little more than an inch in width, and with a rug hook draw up the end at a point an inch and a half from the margin. Here make a cluster of three half-inch loops and around this cluster bring up a circle of long loops; there will be at least eight. If the strip you have selected is too short to complete the circle, draw it up in the centre, then proceeding around the circle as before. If the strip is too long, draw it up in the centre and cut if off, rather than continue it to another flower. Next, select a bit of bright or contrasting colour and with more half-inch loops, fill in every space between the first cluster and the outer circle of petals (Fig.4). Then shear off the top of every loop in this centre. The last and perhaps the most interesting step is to sew the petals in place by a stitch at the end of each, using strong thread or string. I use string, as the stitches are not visible on the upper side. Pass the needle or bodkin through each loop separately, drawing it out to the full length in a pointed shape and so fasten that the burlap foundation will be completely covered without crowding and losing the individuality of the flowers. Should any spaces appear they may well be filled in with short clipped loops of green to simulate a background of leaves.

Fig.6 clearly demonstrates how the flowers are dovetailed together in the design. They can be given form and shape by using a selection of graduated loops for the petals and an oval centre in place of round. This last grouping was made of light flowers – from cast-off "undies" and stocking legs – on a background of clipped dark blue.

My way of working is to draw in a number of flowers, placing them at the proper distances (they can easily be gauged by the eye), then fill in and clip the centres and sew the petals in place as the spirit moves me.

Above: Silk panel applied to grey polyester with the silk strips being hooked. (Mary Day Silk Painting Studio)

Above: Joan Swift, *The May Tree.* Tree hooked; sky background painted on hessian; other details embroidered. (30 x 28in)

Above: Various gauges. Cardboard gauge showing cutting down open centre. Photo Christine Carpenter.

Left: Small hooked cushion, using various kinds of velvets.

Nicky Hessenberg, 1996. Detail from prodded hanging 'Shoreline'. Variety of fabrics with seashells stitched on.

The finished product is soft and comfortable for a chair seat or back, substantial enough for a serviceable rug, dainty enough – provided the material has been carefully selected – for a cushion that will stand hard usage and retain its good looks indefinitely. It is the speediest way I know of to cover a section of burlap and convert it from prosaic feed-bag to an attractive bit of home furnishing.'

FURTHER VARIATIONS

Try wrapping a thread or strip of material with another transparent material and hooking the two together: the thread shows palely through the transparent material, thus giving a diffused effect. The small seascape panel illustrates where chenille has been used in this way. Embroidery stitches have been used to cover the rest of the base fabric.

When making a wall hanging, or a cushion cover, or something that is not going to take a lot of wear, you can use a coloured even-weave material or hessian as your base fabric and just hook the main picture. The unicorn panel illustrates this. Coloured hessian can fade, so keep it away from strong sunlight.

Above: Close-up of panel.

Left: Falling leaves. Small panel showing hooky and proddy techniques. (Ann Davies). Photo Christine Carpenter.

Those interested in silk painting might wish to use a silk painted panel as a starting point for a wall hanging or cushion cover. In the illustration is a small silk-painted panel which has been stitched over padding and applied to grey polyester. This part of the work can also be quilted. Silk fabric was also randomly dyed with colours influenced by the panel, then cut into narrow strips and hooked, using a fine hook.

There are many other variations on this theme possible, and, as with anything else, it is always rewarding to experiment: it really is surprising that a simple loop can produce such a variety of different effects.

PRODDY

This traditional technique produces a shaggy pile similar to that made by the rugger. It is worked from the reverse side of the fabric, and you will find that the pile will produce a diffused effect, unlike the definitive lines that can be obtained with the hooking technique.

Use a wooden or metal prodder, and small pieces of material. The piece ends can either be cut straight across the width or at right angles to the straight grain. Although this technique can be worked without a frame, many workers find it easier to work with one. The base material can be fine or coarse hessian; if you opt for fine hessian you need not cut your strips so wide.

Right: Virginia Creeper:
Proddy hanging, using
dyed woollen blankets.
(Ann Davies)

Right: Close-up of the
hanging, showing the pile.

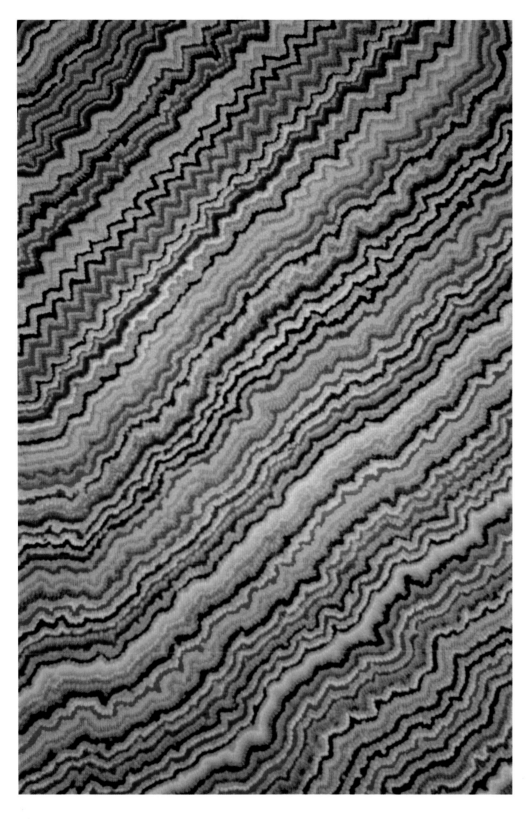

Left: Ann Davies, Hooked rug, 1993. Using up scraps of material left over from other projects.

Preparing your Materials

Cut your strips. Close-woven material lends itself better to proddy technique than very loose material. You do not have to cut each strip to the right length individually, but proceed as follows: first, determine how long you want them to be: this is usually about 3–5in in total, to give a pile of 1½–2in depth. Then make yourself a gauge using a strong piece of cardboard: fold this in half lengthways. Wrap your strips round and round the cardboard singly – do not overlap them – and once this is completed, take a sharp pair of scissors and cut through the strips at the open end of the gauge. A matchbox held lengthways also makes a good gauge for 4–5in strips; or a piece of dowelling with a diameter of about 1in, with a heavy score line along one side, can be used. Occasionally one comes across the old-fashioned wood gauges once used for cutting rug yarn; these can be used if they are deep enough.

Mark out your design on the reverse side of your base fabric, allowing margins. If working without a frame you can turn the margins down on the wrong side and prod through the double thickness up to the edge of the rug.

Proddy Technique

Always start from one side of your work and work across.

1.   Push your prodder firmly down into the backing, making a large hole. Take a piece of your cut material and, using your prodder, push one end into the hole (always the width and not the length).

2.   With your fingers under the hessian, feel for the end of the strip and pull it half way through, so that half of the strip is above the hessian and half below.

3.   Leave about two threads of the mesh, and make another large hole with the prodder. Then push the other end of the strip through the hole, so that it is in effect level with the first end, producing a U shape. Always push an end through the hole, do not try to push the length through.

4.   Take the prodder again and enlarge the first hole, and repeat the above steps exactly so that two ends end up in every hole; this makes a very firm pile.

If the fabric is very thick it may be advisable not to use the same hole twice, but to use the technique singly, that is, leaving a couple of threads between each U shape. Single prodding was used to produce the effect of a hydrangea head as shown in the sample being worked.

As you work and build up the pile you may find it difficult to locate which strip you are pushing through, but if you keep your prodder down against the strip you have just pushed in, you will be able to locate it more easily.

As you will see from the panel illustrated, both hooky and proddy techniques have been incorporated in the design. Some of the ends of the pieces are cut straight across and some at angles. This would not be practical as a rug, because the two techniques would wear differently.

Opposite: Hydrangea head, using a variety of shot silks and the single proddy technique. (Margaret Walker) (Photo. Christine Carpenter)

4 Alternative Rug-Making Techniques

THE RUGGER

The first mention of this tool was in rug-making and needlecraft publications of the 1930s. It was called Brown's Patent Rugmaker, and this logo was often imprinted on the lever handle. A similar version of the tool was also produced by other manufacturers. It is a technique which can be used for rugs, wall hangings, cushions, seat pads, or incorporated with other textile techniques. The principle of this tool is that it has a double-strength spring and a lever; it is held in the palm of one hand, and the lever is operated by the thumb. You do not work on a frame.

There are still many original ruggers about, to be found in workboxes, junk shops, car boot sales and charity shops. Some are still usable, though the chances are that the spring will not be strong, or might have gone completely. If this is the case, take a strong safety pin or kilt pin, and break off the head but retain the spring; then using a pair of pliers, follow the placement of the pin on the old rugger. This will give it a new lease of life. If, however, you find that the point has blunted with use or has become crooked, then it would be better to put the rugger away as a memento and buy a modern one. The modern rugger is much stronger than previous tools as it has a spring on each side of the lever.

Your base material is usually either coarse hessian, or 3.3 squares to 1in mono rug canvas. When using the rugger

method the finished appearance produces a diffused effect, similar to the shaggy pile achieved by using the prodder.

Topical Tips

When assessing the size of the base material required, allow about 2in more than the size of the rug for turning in hems. If you turn the hessian in before you start work, the hem can be taken up into the work as you thread the strips. Alternatively, work your rug, and then turn the hessian to the reverse side to

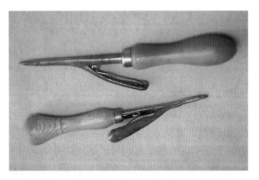

Below left: Old Ruggers.

Below right: Modern rugger showing a spring on each side – not down the centre as in the older models.

Bottom: Rugger being pushed through several threads of coarse hessian, and open ready to receive material. Photo Christine Carpenter.

Opposite: Close up of locker hooked panel illustrated on page 69.

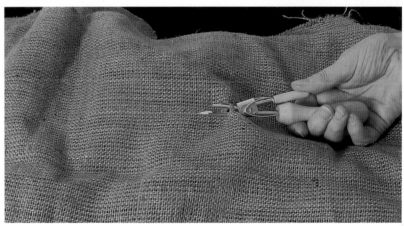

Top right: Chair seat on canvas (Ann Davies).

Bottom right: Close up of pile.

make the hem; if using canvas, turn the canvas down to the back about two or three squares and work through the double thickness. You can if you wish, after working the rug and before turning the hessian down, sew carpet binding all round, on the front of the work close up to the final row worked, and then turn it down to the reverse and sew it down, using a herringbone stitch.

It is a matter of choice whether you line the back of the rug, but if you do so, bear in mind that any grit held in the base of the rug will act as an abrasive.

You can use a variety of fabrics with this method, but wool or cotton fabric or thick yarns are the materials usually chosen. Cotton strips should be cut wider than wool fabric ones.

Preparation and Technique

Cut or tear your rags into strips about 1in wide, depending on the thickness of the fabric, and then cut them into lengths of 4–5in: use a gauge to cut the lengths (see Proddy, Chapter 3). For variety you can cut the tips of your strips into points, but you would have to do this individually on each strip.

1.   Hold the rugger in your right hand (reverse the holding instructions if you are left-handed) and push its tip down

Below: Rugger bringing piece of material through the hessian. Photo Christine Carpenter.

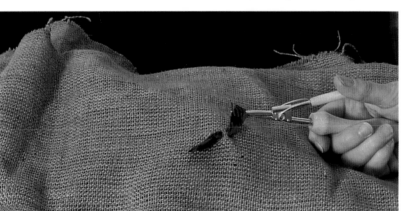

into the base canvas or hessian. Let the tip go under a few threads, then bring it up from the back to the front, making sure that the shaft of the rugger is well clear of the base material. If using canvas you would put the rugger into one square and back up the next. Do not leave any gaps. Again, work in the previous holes unless your material is very thick.

2.   With your thumb on the lever operator, open the tip to its fullest extent. In your left hand hold a strip of the cut material and let the lever close over one short edge of the fabric. Pull the rugger back until half of the rag strip has come through the hessian or canvas. Release the end of the strip by opening the lever.

Left: Flowers. Small rug using microwave dyed blanket, and other woollen fabrics, using the rugger technique. (Ann Davies). Photo Christine Carpenter.

3.   To make a really firm pile, when you take up the next strip put the rugger into the previous hole you have made, thus having two ends in every hole. By using this method the strips are pushed up, and the tendency to produce a ridge is obviated.

4.   If using very thick fabric strips you may find that the base canvas will tend to 'hump'. In this case use the strips singly, and don't put them into the previous hole. Repeat the whole process, working into every square if using canvas, or, if using hessian, about three to four threads from the first strip.

This technique can be used in a variety of ways. Illustrated on the previous page is a chair seat worked on canvas mesh.

LOCKER NEEDLE OR LOCKER HOOK

Locker hooking uses a tool which at one end looks similar to a crochet hook, and at the other has a large eye similar to a darning needle. A length of wool, or soft thread such as dishcloth cotton, is threaded through the needle end of the hook and is drawn through the centre of loops which have been worked and left on the hook, thus 'locking' them in place. The first mention of this technique appeared in print in the 1930s. The material for the loops can be anything, but those most often used are cotton fabric, or woollen yarn (either man-made or home-spun), or unspun fleece pulled into lengths; silk fabric also works well. With this technique the strips can be cut on the straight or on the bias.

     This method is usually worked on a 3.3 to the inch rug canvas, although it can also be worked on 10oz hessian or grey polyester which gives more freedom of design. Initially it would be advisable to use rug canvas. There are smaller locker needles suitable for use on finer canvas – five squares to the inch and sometimes even seven – and with finer strips of material or yarn, but the larger needle is the one most generally used for rugs.

Topical Tips

Before you begin, decide on the size you want your completed rug to be, then

Above: Locker needles.

Right: Whipped and crocheted edges. Photo Christine Carpenter.

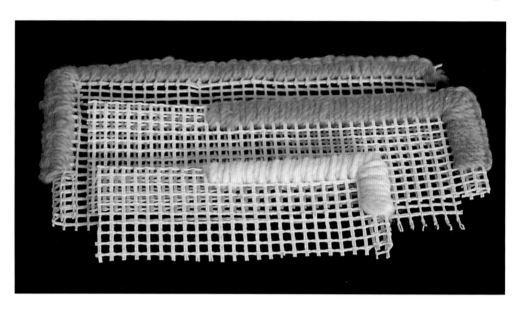

turn down two or three rows of canvas on the right side, carefully matching up the squares. The cut ends will then be hidden in the final pile. Mitre the overlap at the corners to avoid excess bulk, but do not cut the canvas as it frays out very readily. Using a sewing machine, zig-zag the two-square turn-down, or sew by hand. The edge can then be worked in yarn, according to the finish required: this might be whipping,

buttonholing or crochet, or the locker hooking might be worked right to the edge over double canvas for two rows.

To whip round the canvas use a thick yarn and suitable tapestry needle, starting in the centre of one side. To do this, put the needle from the reverse of the canvas to the front. Bring up the end and lay it across about four squares. Work over this. Move one hole to the left and bring the yarn back to the original

Right: Loops being made with the locker needle. Photo Christine Carpenter.

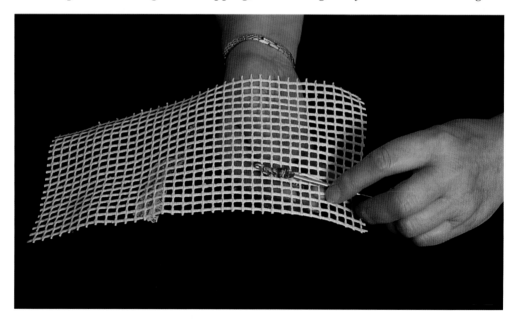

Left: The locker needle picking up the material on the reverse of the work. Photo: Christine Carpenter.

hole. Then move three holes to the left and bring the thread up. Then back two and bring the thread up, working over the stitches in the corners. Crochet stitches also work well for these edgings, working over two squares with big loose loops.

Designs can be marked on the canvas with a felt-tip waterproof pen. Square charted designs tend to lend themselves to this work, for example needlepoint, cross stitch and knitting patterns. You use them in the same way as any other charted designs – one square equals one loop.

Locker Hook Technique

Cut your strips ensuring that they are wide enough to fill the holes and cover the canvas. You work into every square.

Thread the eye of the locker needle with the locking thread you have chosen, about 2m in length. Secure one of the ends of the thread to the canvas, at the edge at which you are going to commence working, by tying a knot onto one side of the square. Insert your hook down the first square.

In your left hand, which is underneath the canvas, hold your strip with one end turned back into a loop. Put the hook under the loop and draw your hook back up the same square with the loop of material on it. Keeping the loop on the needle, and always keeping your needle parallel to the canvas (do not hold it like a crochet hook or you will get distorted loops), put the hook into the next square of

Above: Two locker-hooked cushion covers worked with hand-spun wool. The lettering is appliquéd. (Mary Bell)

Right: Sketch of how to join fabrics (with thanks to Mr and Mrs Bowen).

Opposite: Chair with locker-hooked seat using silk strips. (Jane Evans)

canvas and, holding the strip of material with a slight tension, put the hook under the material and bring it back through the same square. Don't be tempted to wrap the material round the hook: you get a much neater loop by putting the hook under the material and drawing it back up.

You now have two loops on the needle. Continue until you have six or eight loops on the needle. Draw the needle and thread through the centre of the loops until all the thread is through. This thread locks the loops and prevents them falling back through the canvas.

When you start again, after pulling the locking thread through the loops, you may find that the last loop disappears through the canvas. To avoid this, hold the locking thread back while you hook the next loop only. If this loop does disappear or is lower than the rest, you can tweak it back with your fingers. As you get more experienced you can get about ten to twelve loops on the needle before you lock with the thread.

When you get to the end of your strip of material just leave the end at the back

of the work and commence another strip as you started the first: with a loop. If using yarn, darn in the ends.

Alternatively you can join fabric strips together by using the slit joining technique, as follows: take two strips of the material you want to join and fold over about 1in at one end of each strip of fabric. Cut about a ½in slit into the fold. Take strip B and bring it through A until the slit in strip B is clear of the slit in strip A. Take the other end of strip B and pull it through the slit on strip B. Then take the ends of both A and B and gently pull them against each other until a knot appears between strip A and strip B. This is a useful way of joining material when using the giant lucet (see below).

If using the joining technique you may to do a little tweaking when you get to the join. If using yarn, on the reverse side twist the end of the old with the beginning of the new yarn for three or four loops, and then cut off the excess.

Renew the locking thread by joining another length of thread to the old one with a firm slip knot or a flat reef knot.

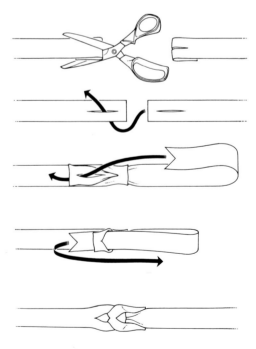

Above: Locker-hooked hanging using fabric and yarn. (Linda Kinnard)

The knot will vanish completely under your loops. Depending on the material you are using for the loops, you might have to slightly ease the knot through. If you are using a very fine material for your strips you may find it easier to join the thread on the reverse of the work using a firm knot.

You can also work diagonally across your canvas, but if you do this you will need to cut your strips wider to fill the squares properly. Also be aware that working a lot of diagonal hooking may slightly distort the canvas.

When you come to the end of the row, push the hook down through the next square in the same row (this can sometimes be into an already worked square). Pull the locker thread down underneath the canvas. Push the locker hook and thread back up to the front through the next square to be worked. A back stitch can be worked to prevent distortion at the end of a row. The first loop of the new row will be made here.

Use the left hand to work from left to right, or turn the work round to continue working from right to left. An interesting effect is produced if the canvas is turned sideways, and 'vertical parts' are worked alongside horizontal areas.

It is advisable to line the rug because of the loose ends on the wrong side. Do this in two pieces, as you would if making the back of a cushion cover, so that the grit can be shaken out.

Making a Frame

You may find that, when working a large piece of rug canvas, it is difficult to

manipulate it at first because of the stiffness of the canvas. You can help to alleviate this problem by making a home-made frame to hold the canvas:

1. Take a piece of wood approximately ½in (1.25cm) thick and 2in (5cm) wide, the length being slightly longer than the width of the canvas to be used.

2. Put a piece of the canvas you intend using on top of the piece of wood and mark out on the wood the centre square; then continue to mark out at approximately 3in (7cm) intervals along the complete length of the wood, being careful to ensure that the marks marry up with the squares of the canvas.

3. Headless nails are then hammered in at each mark, so that they protrude approximately 1½in (3.5cm) above the wood.

4. The completed frame is then clamped to a table by two G clamps.

5. To protect yourself from the nails, put a strip of firm foam rubber over the nails.

When the larger canvas becomes unwieldy, roll it up and use large safety pins or kilt pins to secure the outer edges together. A small card table (or similar) helps take the weight of the rolled-up canvas.

You will see from the pictures that there are two pieces of conventional locker hooking, one using cotton strips

Above: Christmas Trees. Locker-hooked panel using cotton strips. (Ann Davies) Photo Christine Carpenter.

Right: Panel with appliquéd calligraphy and locker-hooked, hand-spun wool. (John and Mary Bell)

Right and below: Braids worked on the lucet using wool and fabrics. (Mary Bell). Photo Christine Carpenter.

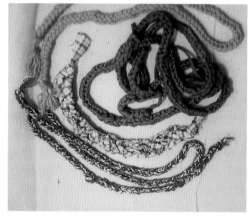

Below: Locker hanging using a variety of fabrics. (Pat Willis)

and the other fine silk strips. A further piece is worked with hand-spun fleece, and the calligraphic areas have been applied (over padding) in spaces left for it when planning the piece. The wording is Gaelic and it is a song used by Scottish tweed makers when fulling the tweed. The two cushions covers have been made using hand-spun wool, with the initial in the centre being applied before the locker technique was used. Also illustrated is a chair, with the seat covered using 3.3 canvas and silk strips.

This technique can be used for rugs, wall hangings, cushion covers, clothing and a variety of other uses; it can be incorporated to great effect with other textile techniques, often with applique.

GIANT LUCET

This tool makes a square cord suitable for a variety of uses such as rugs, edgings, tie-backs and handles for bags. It is called a 'giant lucet' as traditionally

only the smaller one has been available for making fine cords. Material or yarn can be used, though yarn needs to be chunky. If using fabric the strips should be cut as long as possible. With woollen material it is best to cut strips about 1in wide with as few joins as possible; if you are using a close-weave, or fairly firm fabric, you can join your material firmly but without creating a bulky knot by using the joining technique given above.

Threading up the Lucet

Thread up the lucet according to the illustration and sketch. It takes quite a lot of fabric or yarn to set it up initially – about half a metre – and in order to avoid wastage you can attach the end of your material to some string or cord, and thread up using the string. You will, however, have to ensure that the actual material or yarn is wrapped round the arms of the lucet before you begin making the cord.

1.	Starting at A, thread up as in the diagram. Hold the lucet in your left hand and pull loop B over thread A. Turn the lucet over from right to left.

2.	Pull new loop B gently to a slack tension at C in the middle of the lucet. Then pull new thread A straight sideways from the left fork for a similar tension.

3.	Lay new thread A across the right fork, and pull loop B over it. Continue turning the lucet from right to left as you work until you reach the required length.

Below: Giant lucet, together with a more traditional lucet.

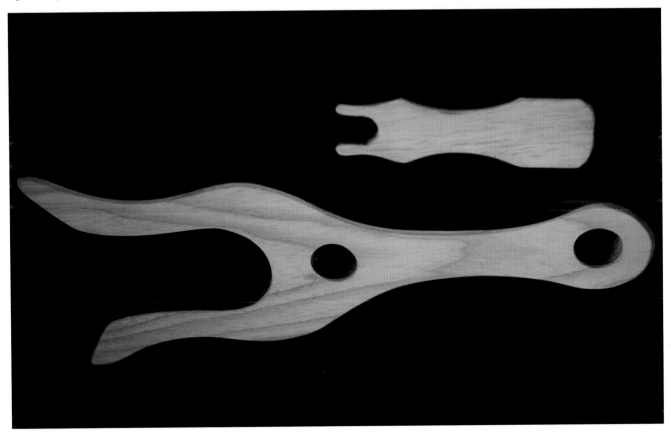

Right: Sketch of how the lucet is threaded.

Far right: Lucet threaded up ready to commence.

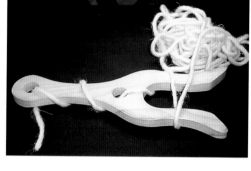

4. Occasionally tighten the yarn or fabric strip through the holes to keep it central in the lucet.

5. Finish the ends by knotting or, if using yarn, binding with thread and fringing out.

It is advisable to stretch the braid by damping it and tying it in a circle, before drying it with a weight attached to it to even it out.

To make this rope into a rug, lay it flat on a table in a coil and hand-sew it together into a circle or oval. Alternatively, lay the strips side by side

Below: Small lucetted rug worked with fabric strips. (Ann Davies). Photo Christine Carpenter.

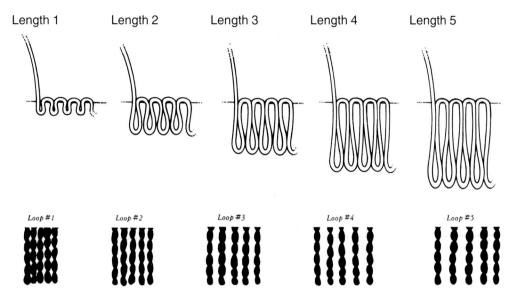

Length 1 Length 2 Length 3 Length 4 Length 5

Top left: Sketch showing the actual size of the length of the loops produced by the Speed Needle. (Rumpelstiltskin)

Loop #1 Loop #2 Loop #3 Loop #4 Loop #5

Left: Sketch showing the gaps (actual size) to leave when using the different heights of loop.

and catch them together. During this stage always keep the rope flat on a table and allow a slight ease as you go round; this will ensure the rug stays flat. Do not be tempted to do this joining with the braid in your lap, or you might finish up with a basket, and not a rug.

A long strip of lucetted fabric could be used as a finishing effect around a hooked or prodded rug.

Recycled woollen jumpers or blankets cut into strips make excellent rugs. If using jumpers, do not take them to pieces but cut round, including the seams.

SPEED NEEDLE

This an automatic loop-making device from the USA which can be used for making rugs, wall hangings, cushion covers, bags and so on; the loops can be adjusted to five different heights, and it can produce some interesting effects. It is sometimes compared to an egg beater, and it does in fact have a handle which, when turned, moves the needle in an up-and-down movement. Both yarn and fabric can be used, but whichever you

choose, most important is that it must run freely through the needle eye. The backing material should be a smooth fabric, not hessian; grey polyester works well, as does linen. It must be stretched very tautly onto a frame, and the frame must be several inches larger than the required finished size.

Setting up your Materials

Stretch the backing material tautly over the frame using a staple gun and staples; trying to keep the threads aligned with the sides of the frame as you do so. When working the speed needle you must ensure that the frame is slightly raised, otherwise the needle will hit the supporting surface: with a small size project you can rest the frame against a table; with a larger size, lean the frame at an angle against a wall and prevent it slipping by putting a weight such as a brick in front of it. With this technique you work on the reverse side and the loops appear on the front.

Place your design onto the material before putting it onto the frame; leave a

Right: Holding the Speed Needle upright ready to commence work (Rumpelstiltskin). Photo Christine Carpenter.

Opposite: Rug using chenille, viscose ribbon and thin-cut synthetic velvet. (Ann Davies). Photo Christine

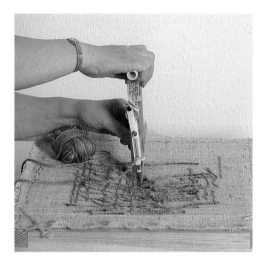

2–3in working margin between the pattern border and the frame, to avoid damaging your needle. The base fabric must always be kept very taut as the needle will not penetrate properly if the backing is slack, and this leads to uneven loops. If the base fabric does slacken off, then tighten it by using more staples.

Thread the needle with the threader provided, ensuring that the handle of the needle is parallel with the main body of the needle. Put the threader into the hole at the needle end and up through the thread guide – this is the small half circle just above the needle.

As it is time-consuming to keep threading the needle when using fabric, cut as long a thread as possible. You can join fabric strips together with purpose-made glue ('Stitchless'); just dab a small amount on each end of the fabric and,

Right and below: Sketch and photograph of the Speed Needle.

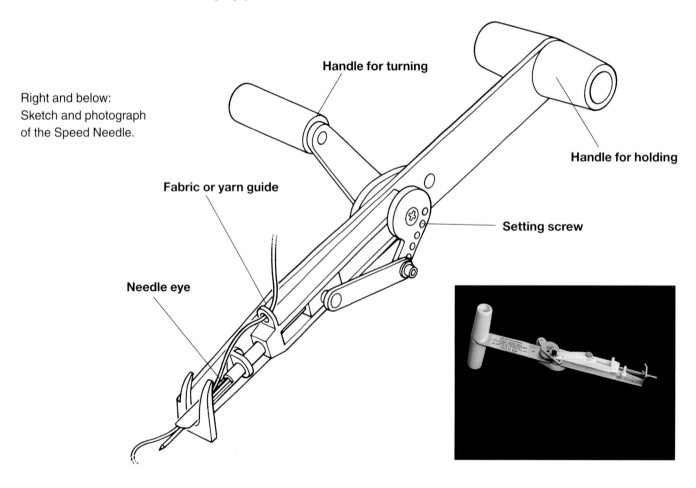

Handle for turning

Handle for holding

Setting screw

Fabric or yarn guide

Needle eye

after a short time, press the two glued ends together. Always ensure that whatever yarn or fabric you are using moves freely through the needle because, if it does not, the previous loops will pull out.

The needle has five loop heights, from ⅛in to ¾in, and these are adjusted by the guide at the side of the needle: 1 equals the shortest height of loop, 5 equals the longest; 1 is the hole nearest to the nut in the centre of the gauge, 5 is the hole furthest away.

Speed Needle Technique

Hold the needle in an upright position, turning the handle in a clockwise direction only. The small V guide at the bottom of the needle must always be pointed in the direction you wish to go. You can operate both towards and away from you by turning the needle around and operating it with opposite hands. Apply a steady, gentle, downwards pressure. The needle advances automatically over the cloth as you guide it along. Do not lean the needle forward, nor look over the top of it as you work – looking to the side of it makes it easier to guide it correctly. If you hold it at an angle it will jump and will not leave an even pile.

To begin, have about an inch or so of yarn or fabric pulled through the point of the needle to the back of the foot. The needle must always be in a retracted, or 'up' position to start hooking. Put the point of the needle into the fabric at the place you intend to start.

Work on a small section of colour at a time: outline the area first, then fill it in. You can work the yarn or material through outlines already worked. The loops can be left as they are, or they can be sheared to give a velvety pile effect. If you want to achieve the latter effect it is advisable to work with a longer loop height to allow for shearing.

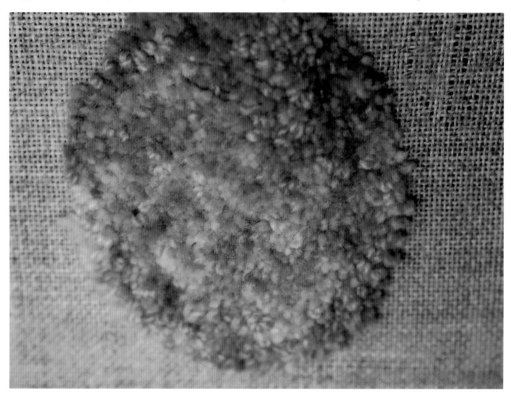

Right: Circle showing different heights of loops.

When you come to the end of a row or wish to change a colour, let the needle come to the surface: hold the end of the yarn or material with your finger pressed against the last stitch to ensure that the loops do not come unravelled, and cut the end very near to the surface of the base fabric; using a darning needle or scissors, push the end to the right side. It will get lost in the pile; if it does protrude too far, just cut it level with the loops.

TROUBLESHOOTING

If your loops are not even on the front of the work, this may be caused by not pressing the speed needle firmly enough against the base material, or the latter may have slackened off and needs to be tautened. Also ensure that your material or yarn is running freely and not snagging somewhere.

Proper spacing between rows of yarn is very important. Rows of loops like No.1 and No.2 on the gauge, which has been drawn to scale, must be close together. Longer loop rows such as No.5 may be up to ¼in apart. If rows are too close together you will use up too much yarn or fabric, and the top of the rug will look overcrowded.

Frequently check your work on the right side for uniform loop length and density of rows. When you think you have finished the rug, make a final inspection on the reverse side to check for empty spaces, and fill them in.

The hooking is easily removed for reworking. Beware though, because if you take the stitches out several times it may weaken the backing. To obviate this, lighten your pressure on the speed needle and 'walk' it as slowly as possible over the weakened area. You would be advised to cover the weakened patch with a small dab of latex in order to secure the stitches. Work on another area while the latexed area dries, and be sure that you do not get the latex on any unworked area; if this happens the needle will not penetrate the backing.

The sample circle is worked from the outside in, using the lowest loop on the outside and the highest loop in the centre.

FINISHING WITH LATEX

Leave the rug on its frame and apply the latex (white glue used for carpet making) to the reverse while the rug is still stretched; only apply it up to the indicated edge of the rug. Latex should only ever be used in a well ventilated room, and be careful to avoid spilling it on clothes or furniture. Pour it into a small pool and spread it immediately onto the reverse of the work; use a square piece of cardboard, or a spatula – a plastic knife also works well. Use the latex sparingly as you do not want it to seep through to the front of the work.

Cover all the loops and leave it to dry overnight. When the backing has dried, remove it from the frame and cut off the excess so as to leave a 3in border. Next, apply latex to this border; let it stand a few minutes until it is tacky. Fold the border in half to form two thicknesses: pinch the hem together, also pinch at the corners and cut across to mitre. Spread more adhesive over this folded hem and into the latex backing. When the adhesive becomes tacky, fold over so that some of the back shows from the right side, and press firmly with the fingers. Fold over far enough so that the backing does not show, but not so far that the rug edge curls.

THE LOOPER

This is a long pointed tool with a hole near the point, and a hollow central shaft set into the handle. It comes complete with a sturdy wire threader so

Right: Showing looper and material being pulled back through canvas.

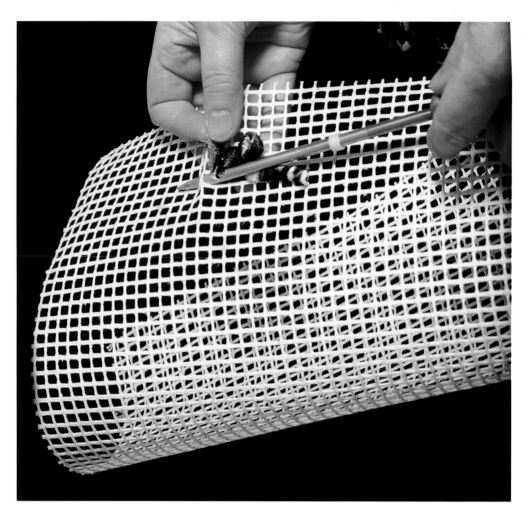

the yarn or fabric can be threaded easily through the central shaft of the looper; whatever material you choose, the strips must be able to pass freely down the shaft. You can use a frame if you want to with this technique, but it does not need one. It can be used on canvas or hessian.

The length of the pile is governed by a moveable stop ring on the shaft. If you find the ring moves during use, tape it down with a small piece of masking tape. The height of the loop is determined by the ring, nearer to the point making short loops, nearer to the handle making long loops.

As the loops are made they are separated by a back stitch; this is an integral part of each loop, and ensures that they stay in place. The technique is worked from right to left (or left to right if left-handed), with the front of the work facing you, horizontally across the base fabric, usually using 3.3 squares to the inch canvas, although it can also be worked on 10oz hessian or grey polyester; the latter allows more movement, and your designs can be freer.

The looper is threaded by pushing the wire threader down from the hole near to the point of the handle into the central tube, where it protrudes far enough for the yarn or fabric to be inserted in the loop of wire. This wire is

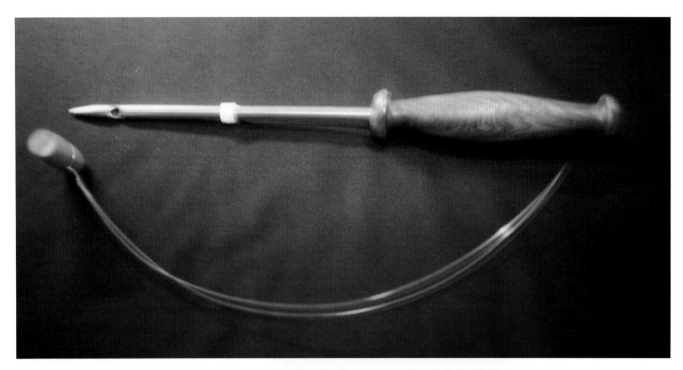

then pulled back up and out of the hole at the end near the point, bringing the thread with it.

Preparing your Materials

First you must decide whether you are going to use canvas, hessian or grey polyester. Mark out the size of your rug or wall hanging: if you are using canvas, allow two or three squares in addition to the required size of the rug, and fold them down to the wrong side, matching up the squares. If you have decided on coarse hessian or grey polyester, mark out the diameter of the rug using a waterproof medium felt-tip pen, and allow a margin of about 2in all round. Turn the excess fabric to the back and work through the two thicknesses; work from the felt-tip line. When using canvas, geometric designs work well, and should be sketched out on the canvas using a waterproof felt-tip pen. Alternatively you can use a charted

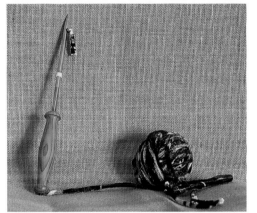

design with one square of the design equalling one square of canvas.

It is helpful to have the canvas caught onto a frame, as detailed in the locker needle section. Otherwise try and work with it on a flat surface, such as a table.

The Looper Technique

The looper is pushed into the first hole to be worked on the right edge of the

Above: Looper, together with threader.

Left: Looper threaded. Photo Christine Carpenter.

Left: Samples using the looper and a variety of fabrics and yarns. (Mary Bell)

row, and then under a thread into the second hole. As it is withdrawn a loop is made, and this loop is held firmly with the finger of the left hand until the tip of the looper leaves the hole. Without raising the looper any further, push the tip into hole 2 and out of hole 3. Continue to the end of the row and cut off any excess yarn or fabric level with the height of the loops. Approximately six times the length of the row is needed to complete one row of yarn or fabric. If you are using a very high loop, then allow extra yarn or fabric.

If alternate rows are worked from left to right using continuous looping, a double-ribbed effect is made by the back stitch lying on one side of the loops. This effect is better when using fabric.

The following materials are suitable for use with the looper: strips of silk about ½in wide, strips of wool ¼in wide, tubular ribbon, two threads of double knitting yarn, three threads of 4-ply yarn, or your own choice of material, cut to run easily through the shaft of the looper. Shaded effects can be created by using more than one colour of fabric or yarn in the looper at one time.

When using fabric or chunky yarn you may find the canvas closing up against the next unworked row, thus making it difficult for the looper to enter. If this happens, skip a row of the canvas to bring the squares back into shape.

The loops can be left as they are, or cut to form a shaggy pile. This is done by cutting the rows of loops as you go – so you work one row and cut the loops of that row.

The point at the end of the looper means that it can be used on coarse hessian or grey polyester, and this gives you much greater flexibility as far as design is concerned; square canvas has its limitations in this area.

Opposite: Rug using the loop technique with a variety of synthetic fabrics. (Ann Davies). Photo Christine Carpenter.

5 Designing, Finishing and Other Hints

DESIGNING

When design is mentioned the immediate response by many people is: 'But I can't draw!'. In fact designing is not drawing, it is being aware of the placing of shapes, the space between the shapes, and whether you find their final placing pleasing to you. Using the word 'shapes' does not mean cut out pieces of paper, but the size and placement of any mass. Our ancestors didn't express horror in the way that we so often do: they looked in the kitchen for saucers, cups, plates and other household items to draw around, using the utensils to make shapes or deriving their inspiration from the designs thereon. They might not have been able to depict animals or flowers accurately, but they 'had a go' and produced something personal to *them*, and that is what you should be doing.

Nor should you immediately ask if there is a 'kit' available. Rather, collect postcards, pictures from magazines, old greetings cards, pretty wrapping paper, whatever appeals to you, and put them into scrapbooks or photo albums. Try to analyse what their attraction is to you: is it the colour, the subject matter, the way in which a particular view is presented?

Start with simple geometric designs or patchwork templates. Take your base material and draw on it broken circles or squares, simple jigsaw shapes or diamonds. If you aren't confident about drawing direct onto the hessian, use cheap white lining paper to work out your ideas. Bear in mind that when designing for a rug, it will be seen from a distance, either at an angle or directly from above, and so it often more sensible to work a bolder design than a more detailed one.

Also consider where you are going to place the rug. Will it be seen from every angle of the room, or is it going to be placed where it will only be seen from one angle? If the former, then you will want a design that can be appreciated from all sides; if the latter, then think of one-way design.

Wall hangings are viewed at a different angle and those looking at them will be able to approach more closely.

Opposite: Photograph that inspired the Virginia creeper proddy rug.

Below: Virginia Creeper proddy rug.

A material itself can help influence your choice of design, and the way it looks can often suggest something – for instance, a flecked tweed could suggest fish scales.

When working the proddy design based on Virginia creeper, I took a variety of photographs depicting autumn leaves and mounted them on a board. This then acted as the inspiration – but no particular photograph was slavishly followed.

The autumn leaves on the long runner were adapted from stencils. Stencils come in a wide variety of sizes and designs and can be used with great effect.

Scaling up your design

When you want to scale up your design to the size of your rug or wall hanging, remember that a good photocopier shop will enlarge your design to the size you require. It isn't a cheap process but it

saves a lot of drawing and re-drawing. Of course, sometimes when it is blown up it is a disappointment, but you can then work on it until you are satisfied with the finished result.

Another way of enlarging your design is by using the grid method. Initially draw a grid with even-sized squares over the original design, place a sheet of clear

Above and right:
Photographs which inspired the Virginia creeper proddy rug.

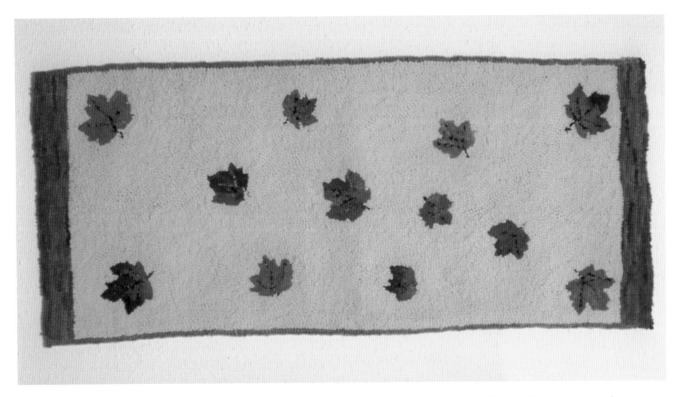

Above: Autumn leaves runner adapted from stencils.

Left: Stencils used in autumn leaves rug (P & Q). Photo Christine Carpenter.

plastic or tracing paper over it, and draw the grid onto that surface. Then mark out the same number of squares in a larger format on another piece of paper, and in each of the large squares, draw what you see in the matching square of the small grid. Alernatively purchase ready prepared grids and use those.

Instead of drawing your larger grid on paper you can mark it out in pencil directly onto your base hessian, using the dragged pencil method. Do not be deterred if you final effort is not to your satisfaction: keep trying, look at what is around you, and do not be put off by what other people say. Visit museums and art galleries; study design books: you will be amazed from where you draw your inspiration. Above all, have fun!

FINISHING AND OTHER HINTS

Finishing off your creation is the most important part. You might make the most eye-catching piece of work but a poor finish can detract considerably from the final effect. As far as rugs are concerned, a good finish enhances the rug's durability, as the greatest point of wear on a rug is on its edges.

Binding the Edges

By binding the edges with a cotton binding tape you ensure that your rug will have years of extra wear. It may appear quicker and simpler just to turn the surplus base fabric to the wrong side of the rug and hem it down, but by so doing, you in fact shorten the life of your rug.

Cotton binding tape is a heavy-duty woven tape available from good haberdashers. It comes in various widths, but the one most used by rug makers is about 1¼in to 1½in wide.

Determine the length of binding you need by measuring all round the rug, allowing a little extra for easing round corners, plus at least 18in extra to allow for shrinkage. Before sewing it to the rug it is advisable to wash the tape in very hot water, and to iron it while it is slightly damp. By doing this you ensure that, should you wash your rug at a later date, the binding will be pre-shrunk and will not shrink round the rug which would cause it to distort.

The colour of the tape should be as near as possible to the colour of the last row of hooking on the rug you are binding. As the tape is only available in a limited range of colours you may wish to dye it so that it blends in with the loops at the front of the rug before sewing it on. (When you dye material for your rug, put the binding into the dye at the same time.)

1. On completion of a rug or wall hanging some people spray their work with a protective spray. Several applications may be necessary, and the first application should be allowed to dry before the next is applied. Just ensure that, if you are using delicate materials or suede or leather, the spray doesn't mark the fabric. Try it out on a small piece of the fabric first.

Binding a Rug

Take the rug from the frame and cut the hessian away until you have about 1¼in spare hessian all round the completed rug. Always commence sewing the braid at a point along the side of the rug, not at the corner. Sewing the binding on by hand on the right side of the work enables you to stitch close against the last row of hooking. Use a strong thread and a backstitch. When sewing the braid round the corners just slightly ease it round, but do not allow too much bulk. When you have completed sewing the braid on, butt the two ends together, and sew them together with a herringbone stitch.

Turn the hessian and braid to the reverse side; before sewing them down you may find it advisable to place a few of the leftover strips of the material used in the project between the braid and the rug. This way, if you do have an accident and need to pull a few loops out, they can be replaced by unpicking the braiding and using the strips to repair any damage. A pair of eyebrow tweezers is very good for easing loops out of the base fabric.

Hem down the braid to the reverse side, using a strong thread and ensuring that no braid is showing at the front of rug, but not pulling it in so tightly that you cause the edges of the rug to curl. Before you reach the corners cut across the hessian to reduce the bulk. Mitre the corners of the braid for neatness and strength.

Backing Wall Hangings

Wall hangings should be taken from the frame and an allowance of about 1¼in of hessian left all round. Lay the hanging flat on a table, and tack the surplus hessian down onto the reverse of the hanging, ensuring that no hessian shows on the front of the work. Take a piece of material slightly larger than the hanging and one which blends with it, and cut it about an inch wider that the completed tacked hanging. Keeping it face down, place the backing fabric on it; centre it and, turning the hem as you go, sew the back all round the hanging, using a slip stitch. Do ensure that you always keep the hanging and backing flat so that you finish up with a flat piece of work and not one which is curved. This is the same method that you would use for lining curtains.

Hanging your Picture

There are various ways of hanging your picture. One is to put heavyweight Velcro along the reverse side of the hanging or picture, and fix the other strip of Velcro to a wooden batten which is attached to the wall. Then press the Velcro strips together. Alternatively, rings can be sewn at intervals along the width of the hanging, and a pole or rod put through the rings. The rings can be ordinary curtain rings, or curtain rings covered with a buttonhole stitch matching a colour in the hangings, or wooden curtain rings covered with a strip of fabric used in the project you are hanging.

COVERING CURTAIN RINGS

If covering a ring with fabric, buy the rings with a diameter rather larger than the pole or rod from which you are going to hang it, as the material can fill up

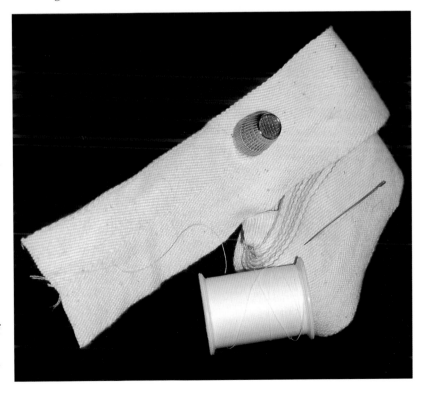

Below: Cotton binding tape, thimble, needle and strong thread.

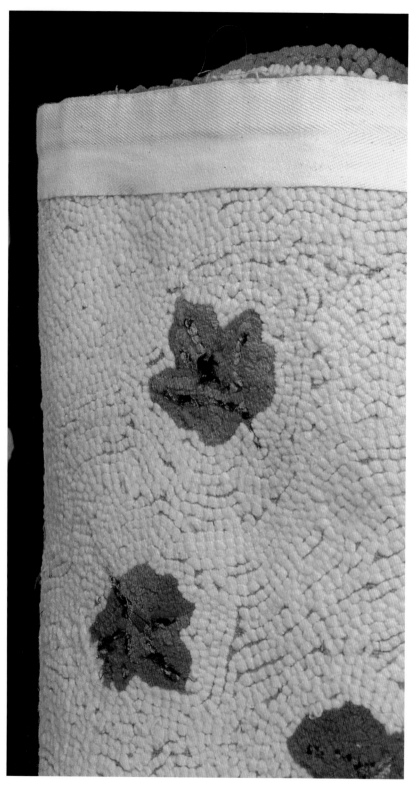

some of the centre space. Some curtain rings come with a detachable screw, and it is easier to wrap the material round the ring if you remove this screw. The actual hole will be covered by the fabric, and so you will need a small awl, or similar, to make a new hole in the ring to re-insert the screw. Use a small amount of PVA glue and spread it along the strip of material, covering it but not soaking it. Take one end of the strip and place it on the curtain ring, and then wrap the strip round and round the ring, smoothing it down with your fingers so that the material lies as smoothly as possible round the ring. Dot an additional spot of glue onto the end of the strip. Hang the rings up to dry – if you place them on paper or fabric they are likely to stick to it, and you will having difficulty prising them off!

Cushions, seat pads and such like, are finished off in the usual way. There are many books available on soft furnishings which will give you plenty of ideas.

Cleaning Rugs and Wall Hangings

First vacuum your rug. Do not wash your rugs if there is any possibility that the colours of the fabric or yarn might run. If you have washed your material or yarn beforehand you will know whether the colours are fast. If in any doubt, have the rug dry cleaned.

When washing hooked rugs use your bath to soak the rug in warm, not hot, soapy water. Use a plunger (sink unblocker), and work it up and down to remove the dirt. Empty the bath and leave the rug in it for a while to allow water to drain from it. Then remove as much water as you can without excessively squeezing or wringing the article. Rinse in warm water again, using the plunger to remove excess soap. Leave it to drain. Remove from the bath and allow it to dry flat. A judicious use of a spin dryer might help in removing excess water, but do not allow it to spin too long.

Proddy rugs are heavy when washed. Again, use the bath to soak the rug in warm soapy water and agitate gently with your hands to remove the dirt. Let the water drain off and then rinse, using warm water. Allow to drain as long as possible to get rid of as much water as you can, and then dry flat. Choose a warm sunny day to do this as the rugs will take a long time to dry. Do not dry them in direct sunlight as they might fade, nor hang them on a washing line because the weight of water could distort the rug and also put a strain on the base fabric. This also applies to hooked rugs.

Hooked rugs can be lightly cleaned by using a brush and sweeping both the reverse and the front of the rug. A vaccum cleaner can also be used on a rug or wall hanging. Do not use a cleaner with a brush-action. You can either use an upholstery attachment set at medium or, if you are not happy at the thought of using the attachment unprotected, put a piece of net over the upholstery head and use medium suction.

REMOVING STAINS

If you have a small stain on your rug remove it immediately by soaking it up with white kitchen paper or paper towels. Ensure that the paper towelling you use is white – with some of the coloured paper towels the dye might come out on the rug. Sponge the area with cold water but ensure you do not get the rug too wet nor scrub too hard.

If you have a stubborn stain, household ammonia and water, or white vinegar and water may remove it. Wipe the solution on the stain and mop up the excess moisture.

There are some proprietary stain removers but first try them out on the reverse of the rug to see whether they are suitable to use on the fabric in your rug.

Helpful Hints

1. If you are not happy at the thought of washing your rugs, they can be dry cleaned, either in a coin operated machine or by a reputable dry cleaner. The advantage of using a coin operated machine is that you can see what is happening to your rug.

2. It is always advisable to sign and date your work in some way. You could incorporate your name and date of finishing into the work you have done. Alternatively, you could embroider or write, using a waterproof felt tip pen, on to a piece of material and sew it into one corner on the reverse side of your rug or wallhanging.

3. When storing a rug ensure that it is clean. Put the rug face down on sheeting (you can, if you wish, spray the sheeting with moth proofing or put a couple of moth balls into the roll) like a sausage roll, with the loops of the rug facing outwards. This prevents pressure on the loops and on the base material. Ensure the ends are completely covered by the sheeting and store in a constant moderate temperature. If the rug is in storage for any length of time check occasionally to see that no moths have got to it, and that it is not suffering any other damage.

Opposite: Reverse of rug, showing edge bound with binding tape and hemmed down.

Bibliography

Rag Rugs, Ann Davies, New Holland

How to make Hand Hooked Rag Rugs, Ann Davies, Search Press

Hooking with Hob Nob, Sarah Wooller, (self printed) Apple Croft Supplies

Rag Rugs of England and America, (history), Emma Tennant, Walker Books

The Complete Book of Rug Hooking, Joan Moshimer, Dover Books

Hooked Rugs (deals with Speed Needle and Punch Needle), Gloria E. Crouse, Taunton Press, U.S.A.

Rugs from the American Museum in Britain (Bath), Shiela Betterton, American Museum 1981, out of print.

The Country Woman's Rug Book, 1930, Ann Macbeth, Dryad Press (out of print)

The Hooked Rug, William Winthrop Kent, Tudor Publishing Co. NY 1937 (out of print)

Rare Hooked Rugs, William Winthrop Kent, Pond-Ekburg, USA, 1941 (out of print)

Hooked Rug Design, William Winthrop Kent, Pond-Ekburg, USA 1949 (out of print)

Rugs from Rags, John Hinchliffe and Angela Jeffs, Orbis Publishing 1977 (out of print)

Opposite: Materials, together with speed needle, hook and looper.

Suppliers

UK

Ann Davies
1 Wingrad House
Jubilee Street
London E1 3BJ
Tel:Fax 0171 790 1093

Supplier of all tools,equipment and
materials mentioned in this book.
Lecturer and teacher. Workshops held.

Art Van Go
16 Hollybush Lane
Datchworth
Knebworth
Hertfordshire SG3 6RE
Tel: 01438 814946
Stitchless and latex.
Dyes, fabric paints.

Blankers
4 Durham Way
Heath Park
Honiton
Devon EX14 8SQ
Tel: 01404 47730
Supplier of blank boxes, and other
articles.

Cloth Market of Stamford
2 St. Mary's Place
Stamford
Lincs PE9 2DN
Tel: 01780 764715
Bargain fabrics including cottons,
wools, silk and microfibres.

Colinette Yarns
Park Lane House
7 High Street
Welshpool
Powys SY21 7JP
Tel: 01483 476356
A wide selection of high quality
specialist dyed yarns

The Cotton Patch
1285 Statford Road
Hall Green
Birmingham B28 9AJ
Tel: 0121 702 2840
Transfer pencils, colour wheels

Colourfull Arts
6 Stretton Road
Sheffield
S11 8UQ
Tel: 0114 2661161
Suppliers of Colour Wheels

Creative Grids
PO Box 207
Leicester
LE3 6YP
Tel: 0116 2857151
Supplier of cutting mats, grids

Kemtex Services Ltd
Chorley Business & Technology Centre
Euxton Lane
Chorley
Lancashire PR7 6TE
Tel: 01258 230220
Comprehensive ranges of dyes.
Advice given on all aspects of textile
colouration

Linton Tweeds Ltd
Shaddon Mills
Carlisle
CA2 5TZ
Tel: 01228 27569
Suppliers of couturier tweeds and yarns

Lowery Workshops
Bentley Lane
Grasby
North Lincolnshire
DN38 6AW
Tel: Fax 01642 628240
Well made frames, and artists' stretchers

P & Q
Oak Tree Cottage
Evesbatch
Bishops Frome
Worcestershire WR6 5BE
Tel: 01531 640001
Wide range of plastic and metal stencils

Rainbow Silks
27 New Road
Amersham
Bucks HP6 6LD
Tel: 01494 727003/fax: 01494 724 101
Wide selection of dyes and associated
products. (Mail Order.)

the paper shed
March House
Tollerton,
York YO61 1QQ
Tel. 01347 838253
Creative hand made papers

Texere Yarns
College Mill
Barkerend Road
Bradford, BD3 9AQ
Tel: 01274 722191
Yarns including silk, gimp, ribbon,
chenille, mohair, etc.

USA

The Color Wheel Company
1337 Donna Beth Avenue
West Covina
California 91791
(626) 919-4767
Colour Wheels

Gloria E. Crouse
4325 John Luhr Road, N.E.,
Olympia, WA 98506
(206) 491 1980
Supplies kits, needles, backing,
adhesive: workshops. Specialist with
the Speed Needle

DiFranza Designs
25 Bow Street
North Reading
MA 01864-2553
(978) 664 2034
Rug Hooking Patterns and Supplies.
Lessons

Cindy Hartman
7240 Mystic Drive
Hudson
Ohio 44236
Tel: (330) 653 9730
Hooks, supplies, kits, lessons

Joan Moshimer's Rug Hooker Studio
Kennebunkport, ME 04046
Toll Free 800.626.7847
Rug hooking supplies and Cushing dyes

CANADA

Spruce Top Rug Hooking Studio
225 West Main Street Street
Mahone Bay
Nova Scotia BOJ 2EO
Tel: 902 624 9312
Rug Hooking equipment, courses.

Rittermere-Hurst-Field
Box 487
Aurora
Ontario LAG 3L6
905 713 2869
Dyes, instruction video, design
catalogue

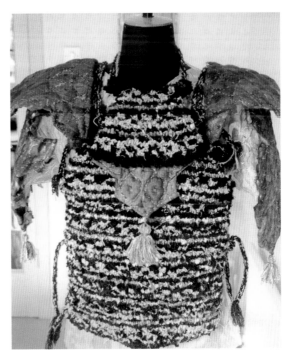

Samurai Warrior:
Inspired by Samurai
armour, the
breastplate and next
piece are hooked
using a variety of
materials including
towelling, cotton
fabric, gold fabric
and cord material.
(Lucy Cook)

Notes on the Contributors

Hilary Ansell was a primary school teacher for over twenty years, returning to college to take an HND in Design Crafts. Now a freelance textile artist and crafts tutor, she runs workshops for art galleries and museums, and spends a lot of time as an 'artist in residence' in various schools, working on large textile panels.
(20 Imperial Crescent, Town Moor, Doncaster, DN2 5BO, Tel: 01302 367896)

Mary Bell was a teacher and lecturer in Home Economics. After bringing up her family she became interested in spinning wool and all woollen crafts. She is interested in all forms of rug making and runs workshops at her country cottage. She has taken a leading role in developing the looper and loves mixing techniques, colours and textures to produce unusual and exciting pieces of work.
(Wensley Cottage, 46 Green Lane, Lambley, Nottingham, NG4 4QE.
Tel: 01115 9312900)

Tessa Miller studied City and Guilds Embroidery and is a freelance textile teacher. She enjoys mixing different textile techniques.
(85 Chinnor Road, Thames, Oxon, O9 3LP. Tel: 01844 214710)

Index